The Doctrine of the Subtle Body
in Western Tradition

The Doctrine of the
Subtle Body
in Western Tradition

AN OUTLINE OF WHAT THE
PHILOSOPHER TAUGHT
AND CHRISTIANS THOUGHT
ON THE SUBJECT

by
G. R. S. Mead

Solos  Press

First published in 1919
by John M. Watkins, London

Third editon
Solos Press
29 Bittles Green, Motcombe, Shaftesbury,
Dorset, SP7 9NX

Distributed in the United States of America by
Atrium Publishers Group
11270 Clayton Creek Rd, PO Box 108
Lower Lake, CA 95457
USA

Printed and bound in Great Britain by
Dotesios Ltd, Trowbridge, Wiltshire.

Foreword

GRS Mead, Hermeticist and scholar was one of the truly great researchers into arcane wisdom. At a time when the 'esoteric' tended to mean little more than table tapping and spirit trumpets, he was busy translating into English the gems of NeoPlatonic and Egyptian philosophy. In works such as *Thrice Greatest Hermes, Pistis Sophia, Orpheus* and *Fragments of a Faith Forgotten*, he almost single handedly put back together the lost esoteric tradition of Classical Athens and Alexandria, which goes under the general heading of *Gnosticism*.

The present work reveals that there is and has always been an esoteric tradition in the West, as well as in the East, concerning the 'subtle body' of man. Echoes of these traditions are to be found in the teachings of the modern Christian church but for the Christian today the soul is an elusive entity, imperceptible yet readily tainted with sin. The word "soul" remains ill-defined and is used to cover a wide range of metaphysical beliefs and concepts concerning both life and a possible after-life. To the modern Christian, the soul occupies something like the role of the king in chess, it is both the most important possession he has, yet at the same time it is weak and vulnerable.

FOREWORD

The doctrine of the soul as a hostage to life, liable to eternal damnation for the transgressions of a mortal body is seldom examined in detail. It does, however, beg more questions than it answers. If we have an immortal soul at birth, why are we not conscious of the fact? What, if any, role does it play in one's life? If it is immortal and presumably conscious before birth, why would it want to take the risk of incarnating as a son or daughter of Adam and Eve, thereby sharing in original sin and requiring salvation by Christ if it is not to spend the rest of eternity roasting in hell? On the other hand, if we have no soul, as many atheists and humanists would assert, how do we explain reports of such things as out-of-the-body experiences and memories of past lives? We can perhaps dismiss the beliefs and teachings of the ages as so much primitive superstition but can we so readily cast aside the evidence of living witnesses? Putting aside prejudice, we can see that in the words of the painter Cecil Collins 'Our modern civilisation is the first not to have a metaphysical basis, it is therefore by definition abnormal'.

If we are to reject the nihilism of the modern age, as increasing numbers of people are doing, then we need to find something secure to put in its place. This is easier said than done because the weight of science and scientific opinion since the time of Darwin both undermines the veracity of the scriptures as historical records of life on Earth and seems to support the mechanistic view of life as the outcome of Godless chemistry. The failure of science to predict still less control such human activities as politics, economics, fashion and love should indicate that not everything which is human can be read in the genes. Human life has a 'subtle' side to it that is something more than biochemistry.

It is just this most human side of life that is, or at least should be, the concern of philosophy. The sciences of biology, anatomy, physiology and medicine treat of no more than the physical vehicle, which is to the presiding intelligence as a car is to its driver or a computer to its operator. The driver of the car or operator of the computer requires that the machinery at his disposal be working properly if his will to travel to a particular destination or to execute some program is to be realised. However, in both cases the machine has no will of its own, for the car cannot choose its own destination and nor can the computer operate outside of the parameters of its programs. The subtle side of life, what makes us human, is related to choice and the the exercise of free will.

But what is free will and what does it mean? What is choice? What is man if he is not really his body or even his mind? Is the soul an abstraction or does it have a real existence in space/time? Is it immortal in the sense that it lies outside of time or does it just have a potential to outlive the physical body for a longer or shorter time before it too turns to dust? Are there several souls, or more properly subtle bodies, that are able to live within one another like Russian dolls and which manifest different properties, not all of them being immortal?

These are not new questions, they have perplexed philosophers throughout the ages and in all parts of the world, not least in classical Greece. The 19th century saw us catch up with and overtake the classical world in the sophistication of our technology (though we would still have problems in duplicationg some of the Egyptian temples and pyramids even today), yet in terms of metaphysical philosophy we live in the dark ages. The classical philosophers, both before and in the immediate centuries after the birth of Christ, left few stones unturned in their pursuit of the meaning of life. It was only after Christianity became the official religion of the Roman Empire and the Academy of Plato had been closed down in 529 AD by edict of the Emperor Justinian that philosophy was subordinated to dogma. Considering that the library at Alexandria alone contained some 500,000 books, it is clear that the philosophical works which have come down to us from antiquity represent only the tip of an iceberg. The destruction of the Roman Empire in the West and the burning of many academic and ecclesiastical institutions by barbarians, followed by the torching of the great library of Alexandria in 640 AD, led to an intellectual dark age. Such books as survived were laregely in the care of the church and therefore excluded writings that were considered heretical. Even so, some philosophical texts did survive in the form of Arabic translations, being translated back into Latin and other tongues after the Moors were expelled from Spain. Still others were brought back to the West for safe keeping after the fall of Constantinople to the Turks in 1453.

This being so, it is surprising how much of the antique record at our disposal has been ignored by both philosophers and classicists of today. It is only quite recently that such NeoPlatonists as Proclus, Plotinus and Porphyry have been treated as important in their own right. Yet even so, many of their writings remain untranslated into English and therefore unavailable to a wider public.

The present volume is invaluable both for the light it sheds on the ancient teachings concerning the subtle body and for providing extracts from unavailable works. It also provides something of a history of ideas, showing clearly how the modern Christian concept of the soul has evolved

from the older, pre-Christian gnostic philoso-
phies of Athens and Alexandria.

*The Doctrine of the Subtle Body in Western
Tradition* is a work that will repay careful study.
It is a very rich and detailed primer, providing
many hints and clues for further study and
research. It is hoped that this new edition will
provide an inspiration to a fresh generation of
readers.

A.G. Gilbert

Contents

Proem

The notion that the physical body of man is as it were the exteriorization of an invisible subtle embodiment of the life of the mind is a very ancient belief.

Conjectures concerning it vary with every stage of culture and differ within every stage. But the underlying conception invariably holds its ground, and makes good its claim to be one of the most persistent persuasions of mankind in all ages and climes.

It is, however, the prevailing habit of the sceptical rationalism of the present day to dismiss summarily all such beliefs of antiquity as the baseless dreams of a pre-scientific age, and to dump them all indiscriminately into the midden of exploded superstitions. But this particular superstition, I venture to think, cannot be justly disposed of in so contemptuous a fashion.

Not only do the acute intellects who upheld it in the past, dispose one to a favourable consideration of their plea that a far-reaching truth underlies this world-wide contention; but I am persuaded that, the more deeply modern research penetrates into the more recondite regions of biology, psycho-physiology and psychology, the more readily will reason be inclined to welcome the notion as a fertile working hypothesis to co-ordinate a considerable number of the mental, vital and physical phenomena of human personality which otherwise remain on our hands as a confused and inexplicable conglomerate.

The notion of a subtle embodiment seems admirably fitted to provide a middle ground on which what, at present, are mutually exclusive views, may be focussed and brought into helpful co-operation.

It may indeed prove to be that mediating ground in concrete reality which is so badly needed to provide a basis of reconciliation between the two dominant modes of opposed and contradictory abstractionizing that characterize the spiritualistic and materialistic philosophy of the present day – the too exclusively subjective theorizing of the one and the too exclusively objective speculation of the other.

And indeed the time seems ripe for a favourable revision of this ancient hypothesis. For already there are many signs that the most recent idealistic and most recent realistic movements of thought are beginning to approximate more closely to one another on a number of important points.

It is beginning to be seen on all sides that the physical, the biological and the psychological activities of man as a unitary reality are so intimately interblended, that no arbitrary selection of any one of these standpoints can provide a satisfactory solution of the nature of the concrete whole which human personality presents.

The old-fashioned materialism, which reached its culminating stage in the latter half of the last century, is now generally discredited, if not dead and buried. The ever more subtle analysis of matter is revealing well-nigh boundless vistas of hitherto undreamed-of possibilities locked up within the bosom of nature, ever more subtle and potent modes of energy that may ere long be made available for our use.

It is now a general persuasion in scientific circles that the static conception of matter, which once reigned supreme, explains nothing. Physical nature is found to be dynamic through and through, even when the method of research still insists upon arbitrarily abstracting the matter of our Great Mother from her life and mind.

If then much of what we shall have to adduce about the nature of the subtle embodiment of man from the records of the most brilliant period of philosophic thinking in the ancient Western world, may seem to subjective idealists and abstractionists too materialistic, they would do well to reflect that we are dealing with what invariably purports to be a corporeal entity, and not with the soul proper, much less with the mind, both of which high philosophy asserts to be immaterial realities.

Man's subtle body is of the material order, but of a more dynamic nature than his physically sensible frame. It pertains to the normally invisible. Nevertheless the latest concepts of modern physics come in as a potent aid in elucidating the most enlightened ancient notions on this subject.

We are not here concerned with the naïve dreams of the primitives, who envisaged it crudely as a thin replica of the gross body, as a diaphanous double of the dense frame as it appeared to their physical senses. Our concern is with the views of thinkers who conjectured its fundamental constitution to be of the nature of a dynamic system of energy, in a manner that is by no means so foreign to the way in which we are now being taught to regard the under-work of all natural objects by the ever more assured results of electronic analysis.

Though then we have the advantage today of basing this ancient hypothesis on the demonstrated concrete facts of positive physical scientific research, we must in justice admit that there is nothing so very original in the concepts we are forced to adopt in endeavouring to explain the facts. We cannot legitimately say they are altogether hitherto undreamed-of novelties in the history of human thought. For as a fact of history we find that innumerable thinkers in the past were persuaded of the existence of a subtle order of matter; it was for them supra-physical, so to say.

It is true that they arrived at their hypothesis by a simpler, if you will even a more naïve, procedure than that now used in our modern laboratories.

They got at it by the analysis of the whole of living

experience without prejudice, by speculating on the phenomena of dreams and visions as well as on the facts of purely objective sense-data, by reasoning on what happened to them without any arbitrary exclusion of everything not given in patent physical perception.

They arrived at their conclusions in what many to-day in their fancied superiority may be pleased to regard as an unscientific fashion. Nevertheless in their endeavour they seem to me to have got at some facts which are still deserving of the respectful attention of the open-minded.

The difference seems to be that what was in the past a speculation determined mainly by biological and psychological considerations, has now to some extent been brought within the domain of exact physical observation.

We are beginning to realize that all our finely drawn analyses of those intellectual abstractions from the full concrete reality of life which we classify as the physical, biological and psychological orders of existence, are inadequate, even when taken together, to give us that sufficient knowledge of ourselves and of our fellows which we so earnestly desiderate.

Life and the concrete reality of living refuse to yield up their secret to the scrutiny of even the most subtle intellectual analysis. No summation of the elements into which human ingenuity has analysed the nature of things, and much less the nature of man, will ever give us again the whole of the reality with which we started.

Nevertheless every effort to explore more deeply the nature of the embodiment of the life of the mind gives us satisfaction in that it is a healthy exercise of the rational function of our unitary selfhood, and is therefore of unquestioned advantage to us as creatures of knowledge.

No excuse then need be offered for the following three essays which attempt to give a brief sketch of the most interesting presentation of the subtle body notion in the history of its development in Western tradition.

They might perhaps be called studies in Alexandrian psycho-physiology; for Alexandria was the chief centre of philosophic culture for the period under review.

If, however, it be objected that Alexandrian is not sufficiently precise a term, seeing that this most famous city of the Hellenistic schools was the meeting-ground of many diverse and the battle-ground of many contradictory traditions and movements of thought, then Platonic may be substituted; for indubitably the views enunciated are throughout dominated by the spirit of that great tradition in its most highly developed period.

Moreover, the consideration of a topic which played a very important part in Later Platonic thought, is not inopportune; for we seem to be entering on a period of a powerful renascence of Platonic studies in their wider sense, and already keen interest has been aroused by some recent publications of first-class merit and importance.

To mention the chief of these only, both on Later Platonism – we have now in our hands the excellent works of Mr Thomas Whittaker[1] and of Dean Inge.[2]

Evaluating the work of the school from a purely philosophical point of view, Mr Whittaker writes (p. 209):

'The Neo-platonic thought is, metaphysically, the maturest thought that the European world has seen. Our science, indeed, is more developed; and so also, with regard to some special problems, is our theory of knowledge.

'On the other hand, the modern time has nothing to show comparable to a continuous quest of truth about reality during a period of intellectual liberty that lasted for a thousand years. What it has to show, during a much shorter period of freedom, consists of isolated efforts, bounded by the national limitations of its philosophical schools.

'The essential ideas, therefore, of the ontology of Plotinus and Proclus may still be worth examining in no merely antiquarian spirit.'

---

[1] *The Neo-platonists: A Study in the History of Hellenism*, second and revised edition, with a supplement on the Commentaries of Proclus (1918).

[2] *The Philosophy of Plotinus*, The Gifford Lectures, 1917-1918 (2 vols., 1919).

The Dean of St Paul's goes further. He boldly declares himself a disciple of Plotinus, and avers that he has attempted to deal with Neo-platonism as a living and not as a dead philosophy – 'to consider what its value is for us in the twentieth century' (ii.219).

What that value is, in Dr Inge's judgment, may be seen by his declaration: 'We cannot preserve Platonism without Christianity, nor Christianity without Platonism, nor civilization without both' (ii.227).

Both of these distinguished writers, however, have paid scant attention to the special subject to be treated. We hope, nevertheless, that what follows will show that in some respects it is still worthy of attention.

It is with this strictly limited point of view that I propose chiefly to deal; for the general subject is of vast extent, indeed of an encyclopaedic nature.

Apart from the vast material setting forth primitive conceits and fancies, as surveyed by the busy industry of anthropological research – the history of the development of the doctrine of the subtle body by minds of higher culture, even if it were confined solely to Western tradition, would require a very bulky volume; while its parallel evolution in Eastern tradition, even if Indian thought alone, in which it reached its most mature expression, were submitted to review, would demand a still more bulky tome.

It may however be of interest to glance for a moment at two of its obscurer aspects in the Occident.

PROEM

The subtle body notion may be said without exaggeration to have been what might be called the very soul of astrology and alchemy – those amazing twin births of human conception which so fascinated the minds of their begetters, and led captive the learned world for so many centuries. The moderns, as we all know, have gone to the other extreme, and cast out the pair of them with contumely as bastards unworthy to company with the legitimate offspring of their eugenically engendered scientific family.

The astral or sidereal religion of antiquity revolved round the central notion of an intimate correspondence between man's psychical and sensible apparatus, or his inner embodiment, and the subtle nature of the universe. The relative positions of the celestial bodies in the aether at any moment were regarded by the most advanced thinkers solely as indices of the harmonious interaction of invisible spheres, with appropriate fields of vital energy.

The ground conviction of astral religion held that there was a subtle organon of great nature, an interior economy of the world-soul. Man's nature was so to say an excerpt from this greater nature; and it was conceived of as a germ or seed as it were of the universal tree of life. Man was the microcosm of the macrocosm.

Soaring far beyond the dross of vulgar horoscopy, philosophic astral theory set up a ladder of ascent from the earth to the light-world.

As it climbed the successive rungs of this scale of ascent, the speculation of sidereal faith rose to ever more sublime heights, and brought such minds as could struggle to the topmost peaks of the mount of contemplation, into communion with the ever living ideas or realities of the spiritual state which energized in the second degree as the formative principles of the world of·becoming. He who could reach to such communion, we are told, had firmly planted his feet on what Plato calls the plain of truth.

So at any rate did the best of them teach concerning the path of ascent, and such did they declare the end of their endeavour to be.

The subject of the origin and development of astrology in the wider and higher meaning of the term, both as the prescientific forerunner of astronomy and as a topic in the comparative study of religion, has of late received much attention from scholars. With alchemy, however, it is far otherwise; and the reason is not far to seek.

The material which astrological tradition offers for our scrutiny is in general straight-forward enough; there is no disguise either of its data or of its dogmas.

Alchemy, on the other hand, has used every device that human ingenuity and perversity could invent to 'camouflage' out of all recognition its subject-matter and procedure. The general impression made on my own mind by a fairly extensive survey of its literature is that the typical alchemist would sooner commit suicide than commit himself to a plain straightforward statement concerning his art.

The alchemists and alchemistical philosophers were, however, by no means genuine enthusiasts for secrecy; for then they would have held their tongues and never dipped a pen in ink. They were on the contrary adepts at self-advertisement, though at the same time their elaborate window-dressing consisted invariably of substitutes for the precious goods in which they professed to deal. Never in the history of human culture has there been evidence of so long continued a conspiracy to disguise the subject-matter and operative processes of an art.

And therefore, in spite of their pretence of conferring priceless benefits by so devious and topsy-turvy a disclosure of the hidden mysteries of nature and of man, they cannot escape the charge, not only always of intentional obscurity, but also frequently of deliberate misleading of the honest enquirer.

The excuse they proffered in mitigation of the charge brought against their procedure was that they were compelled so to act in order to safeguard the inner mysteries of their craft from profanation at the hands of the vulgar, the curious and the unworthy. But this plea cannot be accepted as clearing them from the accusation of thereby also at the same time piling up stumbling-blocks in the way of the serious, the earnest and the worthy.

Doubtless knowledge, especially of the subtle forces of matter and activities of life and mind, gives power; and possession of power is invariably abused by the unregenerate and degenerate. But the antidote to such abuse of power is the still deeper knowledge of regeneration; and this is especially, and contradictorily enough, what the best of our alchemists professed to possess as their central secret.

There were apparently four phases of transmutation – physical, psychical, vital and spiritual in the high sense of the last term. There can be no doubt that bungling experiments on one's own body, life and mind are fraught with great danger. But in every pursuit of knowledge risks must be taken, if there is to be any progress.

The *gravamen* of the charge against the alchemists is that their elaborate 'camouflage' increased the risks and led the vast majority of the inexperienced into greater difficulties than they would have had to face if the way had been made clear for them by frank and straightforward statements.

I do not propose to enquire whether in the lowest phase of the art any of its practisers really succeeded in making gold or discovering a physical elixir of life, if indeed such a notion as the latter is not a patent contradiction in terms.

Chemistry, as we all know, has dethroned alchemy from its once high estate and exiled it from the realm of science, just as astronomy has superseded astro-

logy and driven it out of the scientific state in contumely.

But even as there was a deeper, more vital, side of
astrology, a subtler phase intimately bound up with
the highest themes of sidereal religion, so there was
a supra-physical, vital and psychical side to alchemy —
a scale of ascent leading finally to man's perfection in
spiritual reality.

Indeed, with regard to the real work of the craft,
its greatest adepts are never weary of asserting that
their elements and metals, their apparatuses and
operations, are all invariably 'philosophic.'

Their earth, for instance, is the philosophic earth
which no man has ever seen.

Their gold and mercury, their black crow, red
lion and yellow dragon, are philosophic.

These are all things subtle — agents and patients,
states and processes, invisible to mortal eyes. The
colours are symbolic states of the unseen life of the
body, indicative of its inner natural transformations,
but intensified, hastened and quickened by the attentive supervision of human art.

And so with their furnaces, alembics, baths and re-
torts; with their fermentations, putrefactions, decoc-
tions and concoctions.

The best authorities strenuously deny that they are
dealing with the vulgar metals, plants or herbs, the
patent birds, beasts or fishes of common sense; with
overt boiling and baking and calcination and the rest.

Their concern, they declare, is ever with the 'spirits' of the outer appearances which constitute the gross bodies of things; they would seek to know and control the subtle and vital formative principles of objective nature. They declare that they are 'per-scrutinators' of the soul of nature.

Here then we see that the notion of a subtle embodiment of the life of the mind is with them a fundamental dogma.

The prime secret of alchemical transmutation was an inner mystery – the purgation and perfecting of this subtle embodiment.

The gross alembic, in which the inner work of transmutation was wrought, was the physical body of man. The fervour of his attentive brooding was the fire which had to be so watchfully maintained and warily graded for the hatching out of the spiritual man-chick from the mysterious philosophic egg of his subtle nature.

Thus the wild riot of symbol, myth and allegory in which they delighted, was intended by the best of them to set forth the sequence of a natural inner process of the life of the soul.

All such puzzling devices, when rightly interpreted, they held, would be found to fit into an ordered whole, which told the story of the development of man's inner nature as it could be intensified and quickened by the deliberate application to it of the knowledge of the greatest of all arts – namely, the purification and reorganizing of man's psychical apparatus and the perfecting of the life of his spiritual selfhood.

There is, I believe, a considerable measure of truth in this contention. But what the alchemists do not explain is why they took so much trouble to disguise and mask so heavily what is best in their undertaking, and to conceal under so provoking a welter of 'camouflage' what had already elsewhere been set forth with comparative simplicity and praiseworthy straight-forwardness.

For their grand secret was the soul-freeing doctrine of regeneration, which as a demonstrable fact of history was undisguisedly the chief end not only of the higher mystery-institutions but of many an open philosophic school and saving cult of later antiquity.

The making public of knowledge concerning this high end of human endeavour, it is true, had for long been placed under the most severe tabus. Everything concerning it was wont to be guarded with jealous secrecy, and gnosis of this order was strictly reserved for the elect, who had first been thoroughly approved by rigid testing of their courage and character.

But, if I am not entirely misled by my reading of history, the widespread spiritual ferment at the beginning of our era shows that the power of this hitherto unquestioned tabu had begun to be broken down, and this, as I believe, because it had not simply been over-ruled by the necessities of intellectual honesty but abrogated spiritually by a more than human authority.

This inner authority of an enlightened conscience was immanent in the outpouring of the spirit of the Lord of life which stirred the hearts of men to their depths and changed the minds of large numbers.

It signified the birth of a new dispensation, and inaugurated a drastic departure from many of the old ways. We thus find it boldly declared that the things which had hitherto been whispered in the secret places were now to be proclaimed on the housetops. There was to be an inner transvaluation of values and an outer change in religious method.

Thus the key-note of a new spiritual order was struck for those who had ears to hear. The sovereignty of the spirit was the burden of the glad tidings: the kingdom of eternal values was foreshadowed, and the realm of perduring ends declared to be man's true goal whatever his station in life might be.

Now if in fact this new order issued from above, if it was really an authentic pronouncement of right reason, if in other words it was a wise and deliberate abolition of the ancient tabu, and a just condemnation of that artificial secrecy which was now recognised by the spirit of man that goeth upward to be a hindrance and no longer a help to human progress – then the vital and moral basis for the future reconstruction of society could be assured only by a loyal acceptance of the new liberty by all classes of the community.

16

'Freely ye have received, freely give' was the watch-word.

And indeed there can be no doubt that when the better way of utter honesty and outspokenness has been followed in full sincerity of heart and openness of mind, as in the case, for instance, of modern science, enormous results have been achieved.

Viewed in the light of the new liberty proclaimed some nineteen hundred years ago, the alchemists, in my opinion, must then be judged to have followed throughout their career a policy of reaction.

No matter how piously disposed many of them professed to be, and some indubitably were, they cannot escape the charge of fighting against the light by obscuring it. For what else did they in general effect by their secretive and deceptive methods than to darken the face of heaven and shut out the sunlight with their clouds of confusing symbolism?

They hid their undertaking with such dense smoke screens that they have no one but themselves to thank for their art still being wrapped in an impenetrable fog of misconception.

Historians excusably fight shy of tackling so obscure and evasive a subject; and so it is not surprising to find that as yet the history of alchemy has met with no competent scribe.

Indeed it is difficult to chronicle, even in its purely external aspects; for the recognized literature of the Western tradition alone is exceedingly voluminous.

As to its origins, I venture to think that one of its most important sources has so far not even been noticed.

I would therefore here add a very brief note by way of suggesting how alchemy in its most characteristic vulgar form may be found to link up with traditions of far greater worth and dignity.

It was somewhere about the eleventh century that the art appeared full-fledged in the West, in a Latin Europe that had long been cut off from all connection with the direct tradition of Greek culture.

It came, as so much else came, by means of Latin translations from the Arabic, by way of the Schools of Moorish Spain, which played so important a part in the intellectual development of Europe after the night of the dark ages.

These philosophers and thinkers of Islām derived their culture in the first instance directly from the schools of Hellas. They got their alchemy in like fashion from the Byzantine tradition of the art.

When nascent Mohammedan culture first met with it, the craft already claimed to be the tradition of the Hermetic art *par excellence*. Egypt was held to be its source and origin, and Egyptian Hermes its revelator and patron.

But is this claim really legitimate? As far at any rate as we can now control such statements historically, this particular pretension of alchemy seems, in my opinion, for the most part to be somewhat wide of the mark.

In the first place I am unaware that any alchemical treatise, or even the hint of one, has as yet been found in hieroglyphic, demotic or coptic script.

As to the genuine treatises of the Trismegistic Hermetic tradition[1] – preserved in the Greek corpus, and the excerpts and fragments associated with the honorific title Thrice-greatest Hermes – they are entirely innocent of alchemy in the way that the Byzantine texts of the craft present it.

The Trismegistic texts know nothing of gold-making, or of the elixir of life or of the philosopher's stone.

These Byzantine Greek texts which have only comparatively recently been collected, edited and translated by Berthelot and Ruelle,[2] it should be remembered, were practically unknown to all our mediaeval alchemists. They do not refer to Greek texts.

If we now take the most authentic group of these documents – that is to say, the only one that contains treatises which are not all plainly pseudonymous – the writings ascribed to Zosimus, who lived in the fourth century A.D. – what do we find?

We find an admired confusion of dross and precious things. We find gold-making, recipes for substitute alloys feigning gold, quaint prescriptions of

---

[1] See my *Thrice-greatest Hermes*, 3 vols., London.
[2] *Collection des anciens Alchimistes grecs*, 3 vols., Paris, 1888.

the workshops of the craftsmen, intermingled with the high doctrines of a spiritual philosophy.

The main burden, indeed, of the exhortations of the genuine Zosimus to his pupil, the lady Theosebeia, is that, if she would know the truth, she should betake herself for refuge to Poemandres – the spiritual Shepherd of men, with whom those who were directly taught of God, those known by the generic title Thrice-greatest Hermes, communed – and baptize herself in the life of the Divine Mind.

Zosimus quotes at length from authentic, and some otherwise unknown, Trismegistic works, and in so doing rises high above the beggarly elements of the gold-makers and fakers.

Why then, we ask in amazement, should a genuinely mystical philosopher, who was clearly a member of some Poemandrist community, mix himself up with what must have been for him so paltry a concern as gold-making?

It seems then only reasonable to reject the gold-making treatises ascribed to our Hermetic gnostic as clearly pseudonymous; just as is the case with others; as when, for instance, we find the great names of a Democritus or of an Aristotle filched to father the sorry offspring of far lesser minds, concocters not infrequently of recipes that are first cousins to the contents of a magical medicine bag.

Though it is highly probable that the few strangely arresting visions of graphic symbolism we meet with in this group of documents, should be ascribed to Zosimus himself, it is well-nigh impossible for one who is a student of the genuine Hermetic treatises, to believe that a knower of the simple, straightforward philosophy and high mysticism of the Trismegistic school could have deliberately lent himself to the tortuous devices and deceits of the most vulgar side of alchemy.

In any case, it is sun-clear that the latter has nothing whatever legitimately to do with Thrice-greatest Hermes.

But is alchemy in any sense of Egyptian origin? It may very well be that in its lowest aspect it derived partly, may be even to a large extent, from the workshops of Egyptian craftsmen.

The higher side of it, in so far as this had connection with all the great traditions of regeneration, may also be sought for in part in the far-famed wisdom of ancient Egypt, though clear alchemical traces are not easy to come across in this direction.

Its definitely characteristic psychical heredity, so to say, is more easily traceable to another source by some clearly marked out channels.

Now the two great wisdom-traditions of antiquity were for the Greeks those of Babylonia and of Egypt.

Let us then set our faces in the direction of all that Babylon so vaguely stood for in Hellenistic days. We shall thus find our quest after the psychical heredity of alchemy leading us to Syria and Hither

Asia, to later Babylonian and Chaldaean sources, blended with Persian Magian traditions.

If Greek genius, in the Hellenistic period, philosophized the ancient wisdom of Egypt, it also philosophized this Irano-Babylonian mystical syncretism.

Indeed, if we except Plotinus on the purely negative ground that the *Enneads* make scant reference to the subject, all of the philosophers of the Later Platonic school, as is well known, took quite an absorbing interest in the mystery-lore enshrined in what were most generally referred to as the Chaldaean Oracles.[1]

In 1894 Kroll proved in masterly fashion that all the scattered fragments of quotations, accepted as genuine and referred to this origin in Neoplatonic writings, were taken from one source. This is a Hellenistic poem which provided the subject-matter of voluminous commentaries by a number of the most distinguished members of the school. Unfortunately the commentaries themselves have now all been lost.

When then we find that men of such high philosophical equipment and critical ability as a Porphyry or a Proclus thought so highly of the contents of this poem, and accepted it as enshrining the genuine dogmas of the ancient and valuable traditions of the wisdom of the sages of Chaldaea, the subject seems well worthy of our attention.

Among other things this famous poem sets forth a

[1] See my *Chaldaean Oracles*, 2 vols., London, 1908, in the series 'Echoes from the Gnosis.'

highly mystical doctrine concerning the nature of the subtle body, and of the soul and mind of man, and purports to reveal the mystery of the divine paternal fire and the secret of the life of the great mother.

It is pre-eminently a doctrine of the living fire and all its works, its transmutations and transformations, and also a manual of theurgical lore and discipline. As such it is obviously an alchemistical treatise in the higher sense of the term.

Here then we have a clearly marked channel leading to one of the main streams of origin of the later alchemical art.

Some of the Christian Gnostic schools, moreover, in like fashion supply us with indications of the psychical heredity of the higher alchemy; and this too not obscurely, but sometimes very plainly, in that they employ a symbolism identical with that of the later art.

For instance, in one form of the so-called Ophite tradition, we find the metals associated with the planetary spheres. And in another we read of the mysterious stone which has its mystical implications set forth by free use of quotations from both the Old and the New Testaments.

But it is in the borderland region, in the link between pre-Christian Syrian gnosticism and the definitely Christianized gnosis, that the clearest indication of the line of descent of the higher alchemy is to be found.

We find it permeating the doctrines of one whom the later Church Fathers looked back to as the originator of all the Gnostic heresies which they denounced in such unmeasured terms – in the tradition associated with the name of Simon the Magus or Magian,[1] a title that connects his teachings immediately with a Chaldaeo-Persian background.

The chief document of the Simonian school which we can now recover from the quotations of the heresiologist Hippolytus, is most probably a later redaction of the gnosis of the Magian teacher, due it may be to the high literary ability and philosophical and mystical insight of Valentinus.

This *Great Announcement*, as it is entitled, presents us with a highly developed doctrine of the divine fire and of the tree of life, and with psycho-physiological speculations which are entirely in keeping with the subtle body theory of psychical alchemy.

It is then, in my opinion, not only probable, but capable of reasonable demonstration, that the syncretic gnosis associated with the name of Simon the Magian, is indicative of one of the main streams of the psychical heredity of early alchemy.

Now this Simonian document tells us that 'of all the things which are, both concealed and manifested, that is intelligible and sensible [or spiritual and natural], the supercelestial Fire is the treasure house, as it were a great Tree, like that seen by Nabucho-

[1] See my *Simon Magus*, London, 1892.

donosor in vision, from which all flesh is nourished.'

Here we have the tradition of a grandiose symbolism plainly connected with Babylonian mystery-
lore and the spiritual side of the Perso-Magian fire-
cult. Moreover, in this connection our attention is
specially called to one of the most striking visions of
the Jewish apocalyptic *Book of Daniel*.

Now this arresting document of the Old Testament, which has so persistently fascinated the minds
of uncritical believers in prophecy for so many centuries, and given birth to the ever-renewed feverish
expectations of so many 'latter-day' sects, has been
shown beyond all question by scientific biblical research to be a late pseudonymous document written
about 165 B.C., as was first pointed out by the Platonist Porphyry in the third century.

It was in 170 and again in 168 B.C. that Antiochus
Epiphanes, the Hellenistic lord of Syria, took Jerusa-
lem, profaned and defiled the Temple and violently
endeavoured to root out the Jewish religion. This led
to the revolt of Palestinian Jewry under Mattathias
and his heroic sons the Maccabees; and thereafter
the name of Antiochus stood for all that was accursed
in the history of the Hebrews.

The *Book of Daniel* is certainly an inspired document of its own peculiar order. It is a polemical
religio-political writing in which is depicted in
graphic narrative and skilful imagery the triumphant
superiority of the holiness of Israel, of the pious seers

of the times who succeeded to the tradition of the ancient schools of the prophets of Yahweh.

This spiritual triumph was ostensibly at the expense of the Chaldaean soothsayers and Magian adepts of the Babylon of the Exile; but in reality the polemic was aimed against the Hellenized orientalism of the Syrian kingdom of Antiochus.

The *Book of Daniel* is the earliest example we now possess of Jewish mystically concealed political controversy, with which national theocratic claims were inextricably interblended, and all set forth in the disguise of a pseudo-historical setting.

It is the typical instance of the nature of that literary 'camouflage' which later on became so common in the Jewish revolt against Rome, and its method of procedure is characteristic of much in their rich apocalyptic literature, in the pseudo-prophetical setting of the Sibylline Oracles, and in no little of the Talmuds.

The political opponents of the Jews were, in the belief of these writers, all without exception enemies of God, and the blasphemers against their religion were the execrable servants of Antichrist. Antiochus was the arch enemy of the faith; so also had been Nebuchadnezzar who had also before him ravaged the holy land and enslaved the chosen people of God.

The Jewish apocalyptic writers and religio-political scribes were adepts in setting forth typically present events in the guise of past history, and in forecasting the future to suit the hopes and ambitions of a people who believed themselves destined by God for world-rule.

Their favourite preoccupation was to depict their race as the chief element in world-history, the protagonist of the world-drama, and to show how all had been predestined on their behalf, by setting forth what had occurred or what was occurring as though it were the utterance of prophetical revelation. The Hebrew language so used might almost be said to be possessed of a prophetical tense.

Now just as the visions of Ezekiel are strongly tinctured with the imagery of Babylonian religious conceits, for he prophesied in that land of symbolic iconography, and was naturally psychically impressed with his imaginal environment, so are the visions and mystical incidents of the *Book of Daniel* replete with a similar tincturing of symbolism.

In it, as we have already seen, we find reference to the graphic image of the world-tree. The two other most striking pictures in the narrative are: the symbolic monster-statue set up by the king who exalted himself to divine honours – that image of the lord of the world whom he would compel all men to worship; and the fiery furnace into which the three pure ones, the pious servants of the true God, are cast.

The gold and silver, the brass and iron, of the typical image of the god of the aeon can be more immediately referred to the chief alchemical metals

27

than to the four astrological ages of sidereal religion.

As to the fiery furnace, which blasts to ashes the servants of the oppressor even though they stand outside it, while the three holy ones, though encircled by its fervent heat, are not only not consumed, but joined by a fourth who in his dazzling radiance is likened unto a son of the gods – surely all this, as soon as attention is called to it, might be recognized as a suggestive setting forth of one of the sublimer stages of that transmutation with which the higher side of alchemy concerned itself?

As far as I am aware, this has not had attention drawn to it before; but I am so greatly struck with this association of ideas, that I venture to think the *Book of Daniel* could with little difficulty be held to bear testimony to a stage in the psychical heredity of what later on became clothed in the motley in which later alchemy so much delighted.

But this is not the last of the footprints leading back to the cave of alchemical origins.

Zosimus categorically asserts that the prime secret of the alchemical art was identical with the most hidden mystery of the Mithriaca.

This indication once again sets our face in the direction of the stream of descent whose channels we are endeavouring to discern.

In spite of Cumont's magnificent labours, I venture to think that by no means the last word has been said on the Mithra-cult or on the mystery-tradition

associated with the name of this far-famed saviour-
god of antiquity.

Nowhere does Cumont in his far-flung researches
connect any aspect of the Mithriaca with alchemy.
He has altogether overlooked this precise and suggestive statement of Zosimus.

Now we know not only that, as has already been
pointed out, Neo-platonists were intensely interested
in the so-called Chaldaean Oracles, but that many
of them were also initiated into the mysteries of
Mithra.

The Mithriaca were closely connected with the
mystery-rites of the Magna Mater. The men were
initiated into the former, the women into the latter.

Both traditions point back to Hither Asia and the
Near Orient. Asia Minor and Syria were the hot-
beds of such syncretic saving cults.

In comparison with the richness of the monuments
and inscriptions, we know but little of the doctrines
of the religion of Mithra.

Of the main myth of the birth and life, of the heroic
deeds of the god and his conquest of the bull and final
triumph, we practically know nothing.

The figured monuments of the myth, the serial
tableaux of the labours of the God, have so far re-
mained without even a plausible interpretation.[1]

There is, however, a liturgical document, purport-

[1] See my *Mysteries of Mithra*, London, 1907, in the series 'Echoes
from the Gnosis.'

ing to set forth the innermost personal theurgical rites, in some ways reminiscent of the far-famed yoga-practices of India, of this initiatory institution of many degrees.[1] This liturgical piece is remarkable in any case as being the only complete ritual of the mysteries preserved to us.

Dieterich, who first rescued the heavily over-written text from the chaos of the Greek magical papyri, had no doubt of its being in its original form an authentic document of Mithraism and as such of the very first importance for a knowledge of its inner rites.

Cumont, however, denies the legitimacy of Dieterich's contention, and the learned world has so far, as far as I know, without exception sided with Cumont.

If, however, I am not greatly mistaken, this un-favourable judgment will have to be seriously re-considered if not quashed. In any case the ritual supplies a hint that may lead to the recognition of an ancient element blended into the syncretism of the later Mithra-cult which might prove to be of far-reaching importance.

In the symbolic scenes of the rite, typical of certain psychical states accompanying the ascent of the soul of the initiand in his psychical passage to the light-world – culminating in his meeting with Mithra him-self, the lord of light and king of the divine fire – there

[1] See my *A Mithriac Ritual*, London, 1907, in the same series.

is one which has of late especially arrested my attention.

It should be remembered that the whole rite purports undisguisedly throughout to be the theurgical process of regeneration, or the bringing to birth of man's perfected subtle body.

At a certain stage in this process of inner transmutation and heightening of consciousness the initiand is said to meet with two symbolically depicted companies of supernal powers in the guise of seven youths and seven maidens. The youths are represented as having the heads of bulls.

Now the familiar myth of Theseus tells us how the monstrous Minotaur – the legendary Bull-man who was Lord of the mysterious labyrinth of that once prehistoric Crete which has now so startlingly reappeared on the stage of history – exacted from the ancient dwellers of Athens a yearly tribute of seven noble youths and seven high-born maidens.

We have here, I venture to think, by no means a chance coincidence.

The ancient Minoan religion, as we now know, was dominated by the bull-symbolism and was also fundamentally a cult of the Great Mother.

I therefore suggest that part of the later Mithra story was reminiscent of the ancient Minoan mythology, and of the legendary lore of a religion of which Grecian history had lost all trace. The subject is, I think, deserving of a detailed treatment and promises to lead the patient investigator far afield.

In any case it is evident that the above items of suggestion, crude as they are in their brevity, open up a number of very important lines of research. A fat volume could easily be written in support of the theses I have ventured to put forward; but for the present I must be content to leave the matter simply as a suggestion of topics of interest that are not unworthy of serious consideration by any courageous pioneer who contemplates writing on the psychical in the element origins of alchemy.

Much more could be written indicative of other lines of search in tracing the history of the doctrine of a subtle body in the West, even though it be in the most summary outline.

But enough has already been said to serve the modest purpose of this proem, which is briefly to introduce a more detailed consideration of the notions of the most accredited exponents of the doctrine in the classical past.

Their views are, I believe, in some respects at any rate, not unworthy in our own day of the consideration of such psychologists as are conversant with the phenomena of psychical research, and not without interest for the general reader.

The Spirit-body

In this short study I propose to consider briefly, and in its inferior aspect only, the theory of the subtle body of the soul, or man's psychical embodiment, as set forth by the philosophers of the Later Platonic school in the generally accepted narrow sense of the name, and by their more immediate predecessors and followers.

Many will doubtless think that such opinions deserve no consideration at all in these days of scientific enlightenment, and that they were better left to well-merited oblivion.

But though it is true that the physical science of those far-off days is now entirely superseded, I venture to think that perhaps some of the notions of these old thinkers with regard to this idea of a subtle soul-vehicle, may be still not entirely without interest to those who are either specially engaged in psychical research or generally familiar with psychic and psycho-physical phenomena. For indeed some of the modern theories put forward to account for certain classes of such phenomena favour a very similar hypothesis.

Let us in the first place pay unto Caesar the things that be Caesar's, and cheerfully sacrifice to the godlets of anthropology and primitive culture by admitting that in the beginnings the soul was apparently believed to be air, and air breath, and breath spirit, and spirit and soul one – just simply air, and pass on to those who thought far otherwise, laying it down as a fundamental dogma that the human soul was a rational reality or activity, an intelligible life, an immaterial essence, and not body or an embodiment or element of any kind.

The loftier side of the subject will be reserved for subsequent treatment, when an attempt will be made to say something about the subtle vehicle or vesture, or better embodiment, of the soul in its purity, the celestial or luciform body, or organon of light, the *augoeides* or *astroeides*, as it was called by our philosophers.

Here we have to deal solely with this vehicle in its obscurer or impurer state, with its inferior relationships – that is, its connections with the animal soul on the one hand and with the body of flesh on the other.

A warning may first of all be given as to terms. We should try to distinguish between living ideas and dead vocables; otherwise we shall be incontinently among the tombs with an amazing 'derangement of epitaphs' to mock us in the obscurity.

The most general term used by these writers for the subtle soul-vehicle in its inferior aspect is spirit (*pneûma*) or spiritual body (*sôma pneumatikón*). But as Paul and others before and contemporary with him use these terms in a more exalted sense, it may per-haps avoid some confusion if in this connection we speak of the spirituous body or spirit-body.

The more attractive view, to me at least, seems to have been that, no matter what changes it might undergo, the subtle vehicle was *fundamentally* one. But this side of the question need not be discussed at present.

Already in such early Christian gnostic circles as were in touch with Hellenic ideas, the confusion be-tween the higher and lower spirit, or the higher and lower aspects of the spirit, was clearly felt. In the *Pistis Sophia*, for instance, we find a strong distinc-tion drawn between the pure spirit and the 'counter-feit spirit,' the latter being apparently identical with the 'parasitic' or 'appended soul' of Basilides and his son Isidōr.

So also with the *astroeides*, the star-like or sidereal body; this must not be identified with the now popular term 'astral body', for the latter bears a closer resemblance to the spirituous body of the Platonists than to their *augoeides*.

Again the spirit-body, or spirituous embodiment, was often called the aëry or ethereal body. But, as a distinction was usually drawn between the lower air (*aër*) and the upper air (*aithēr*), ethereal should per-haps be reserved for the celestial state of this psychi-cal vehicle.

Occasionally it was spoken of as 'nature' – that is,

the 'nature' of the physical body. And after death it was known as the image (*eidōlon, imago, simulacrum*) or shade (*skia, umbra*).

Sometimes it was referred to as the subtle or light vehicle of the soul, to distinguish it from the gross, dense, solid or earthy body, which was often called the 'shell', or shell-like body or surround, in reminiscence of the famous phrase of Plato in the *Phaedrus* (250c.): 'We are imprisoned in the body like an oyster in its shell.'

Here again confusion may arise for the unwary, for the 'image' has of late been sometimes called the 'shell'.

It must, however, be always clearly understood that, for our philosophers, spirit in this sense is subtle body, an embodiment of a finer order of matter than that known to physical sense, and not soul proper. By body, moreover, is not meant developed and organised form, but rather 'essence' or 'plasm' that may be graded, or as it were woven into various textures. In itself unshaped, it is capable of receiving the impression or pattern of any organized form.

The soul proper, on the contrary, is thought of as utterly incorporeal. Psychic life is classified according to its manifestations in body, but is not itself body.

The most general classification is threefold: (1) vegetative, as in plants and in the physical bodies of animals and men; (2) irrational, as in the spirituous bodies of animals and men; and (3) rational, in man only.

Man has thus, when incarnate, not three souls, but three grades of soul or life – namely, vegetative, irrational and rational.

Let us now turn to our documents, first of all glancing through the literature handed down under the aegis of Thrice-greatest Hermes.

The Trismegistic tractates, though deeply tinged with Platonism, can hardly in strictness be called Later Platonic, according to current opinion; for the larger portion of them may securely be placed earlier than Ammonius Saccas and Plotinus (in the third century), who for so long have been considered to be the founders of the Neoplatonic movement proper. The Trismegistic tradition can, however, safely be said to have been one of the most immediate predecessors of the Neoplatonic 'chain'; it indubitably links up with it as an integral part of the Platonic movement.

In this literature we find the doctrine of the spirit already well developed, and that too both in its spiritual and spirituous aspects. It is with the latter solely however that we are here concerned.

From one of the earliest tractates, 'The Sermon of Isis to Horus' (15; iii.200[1]), we learn that spirit is, as it were, of the nature of a quintessence or unitary

[1] The second references are to my *Thrice-greatest Hermes*, 3 vols., London, 1906. (Reprinted 1964).

element over against the gross elements of the physical body.

The 'mixture' of the dense body 'is a union and a blend of the four elements; and from this blend and union a certain "vapour" rises, which is enveloped by the soul, but circulates within the body.'[1]

It is the medium between the soul and the gross body, and so is said to partake of the nature of both. The exposition is set forth, perhaps unavoidably, in spatial terms and material imagery.

Both the spirit and the body, it is to be noted, are *in* the soul, and not the soul *in* the spirit.

Elsewhere, however, in 'The Key',[2] the soul is spoken of as being vehicled in, or on, the spirit. But as the soul is said to use the spirit not *as* its envelope but only 'as though it were' its envelope, there is no real contradiction.

We are further told, in the same passage, that 'spirit pervading [body] by means of veins and arteries and blood, bestows upon the living creature motion.'

The writer, however, insists that blood is not soul or life 'as some think'. Blood is the vehicle of spirit,[3]

[1] Cp. Ex. xv.2 (iii.66): 'And from the union [lit. breathing-together] of these four is spirit born.'

[2] C. H. x. (xi.) 13, 17 (ii.149, 152).

[3] Cp. *Vita Homeri* (p. 341): 'For Homer knew that blood was the food and aliment of spirit.' Diogenes Laërtius, therefore, seems to be confusing terms when (viii.31, p. 518) he attributes to Pythagoras the opinion 'that the *soul* is nourished by blood'. It is true that Porphyry also says (*De Ant. Nymph.*, p. 257, ed. Nauck) that 'souls

and it is spirit that conditions the 'living creature'.

Thus in 'The Perfect Sermon', vi.3 (ii.318), it is said that 'spirit with which they [animal bodies] all are filled, being interblended with the rest [presumably the four elements], doth make them live.'

This is based on a general principle laid down in the same treatise, xvi.3 (ii.336) – namely, that all things in the cosmos are 'made quick' by spirit, and that this unitary spirit, quintessence or 'one thing', is as it were an 'engine' or 'machine,' i.e. an *organon*, subject to the will of God – and therefore in man, to man's will.

Moreover this same spirit is the common sensory. Thus in Ex. xix.3 (ii.81f.): 'The sensible – the spirit – is that which doth discern appearances. It is distributed into the various sense-organs.' A portion of it becomes 'spirituous sight', or 'spirit by means of which we see,' and so for the rest of the senses.

If this spirit, in the case of man, 'is led upwards by the understanding', then it discerns sensibles – that is, apparently, what are called objective realities: 'But if it is not, it only maketh pictures for itself' – that is, is given over to phantasy or imagination (*phantasía* or *tò phantastikón*).

---

in generation delight in blood and moist seed', adding that 'by means of blood and out of the hematic fluids is the procreation of flesh'; but delight is not nourishment. As Goethe said, 'blood is a quite peculiar fluid', and it is worth noting in this connection that the bond of blood-relationship plays the chief role both in primitive ancestor-worship and also in most modern 'spirit communications'.

We learn, however, from the myth of the imprisonment of the souls in fleshly bodies as a punishment, that when thus incarnate they lose the direct vision they previously enjoyed, and their sense becomes dim. They can no longer see heaven and their starry brethren in their true forms. They complain that their bodies are now 'watery spheres', and their organs of vision 'windows not eyes' (K. K. 21; iii.109).

All of this may be taken to reflect the Platonized dogmas of syncretic mystical Alexandrian psychology or psycho-physiology, tinged with Egyptian and perhaps Persian, that is Chaldaeo-Magian, notions.

The Later Platonic school proper boasted that it continued the direct tradition of Orpheus, Pythagoras and Plato.[1] But what we may call revived or Pythagorean Orphism spells already for the latest scholarship a decided 'Oriental', that is probably Babylonian-Persian, influence. And this Orphism strongly influenced Plato also in his myths.

Omitting early Orphism, however, is there anything from the later period that may help us in our present enquiry?

If the graphic vision of the after-death state, an arresting rumour of the hither hereafter, handed on or redacted by Plutarch at the end of the first century,

---

[1] See my *Orpheus*, London.

in his treatise *On the Delay of Divine Justice*,[1] and thought by some to underlie the general idea of Dante's *inferno* and perhaps *purgatorio*, can be held to be based on the doctrines of Neopythagorean Orphic mystagogy, we have something to our purpose. In any case the eclectic Plutarch, though difficult to label, has been classed by some as a Platonist or even as a Neoplatonist, and therefore may legitimately come into our purview.

Though the word 'spirit' is nowhere mentioned, the idea is there; for the deceased are said to be surrounded with a 'flame-like bubble' or envelope. These surrounds are described according to their purity or impurity as follows:

'Some were like the purest full-moon light, emitting one smooth, continuous and even colour. Others again were quite mottled – extraordinary sights – dappled with livid spots like adders; and others had faint scratches' (xxii., p. 564D).

The discolorations and the passions that give rise to them are described, and it is explained that 'it is in earth-life that the vice of the soul (being acted upon by the passions and reacting upon the [? spirit-] body) produces these discolorations; while the purifications and corrections here [*sc.* in the after-death state] have for their object the removal of these

---

[1] *De Sera Numinis Vindicta*; for a translation and commentary see *The Vision of Aridaeus*, 1907, in the series 'Echoes from the Gnosis', London.

blemishes, so that the soul [the spirit rather] may become entirely ray-like (*augoeides*) and of uniform colour' (p. 565c).

We will now turn to the opinions of the Later Platonists proper, and especially to the views of Plotinus, and of his disciple, editor and assiduous commentator, Porphyry, who are generally held to be the most sober philosophers of the school, though indeed of late their successors also are being recognized as possessed of an excellent philosophical equipment. And yet, strangely enough, neither of them was a Greek, for Plotinus was in all probability an Egyptian and Porphyry unquestionably a Syrian.

Though the school technically ends with Damascius (also a Syrian), the last occupant of the Platonic *kathedra*, who retired to the court of the Persian King Chosroës, when the Christian Emperor Justinian closed the Pagan schools of philosophy in 529, its influence still survived; for John Philoponus, the last of the Alexandrian philosophers, whom we shall bring into court later on, is saturated with its views.

Philoponus flourished at Alexandria in the first half of the seventh century, and is renowned for his learning and his elaborate commentaries on the works of Plato and Aristotle. In the now generally discredited story of the burning of the Alexandrian Library by Amru, the general of Omar, it is said that it was to Johannes the Laborious that the familiar question about the Qurān and the contents of the world-famed library was put.[1]

Plotinus holds that all souls must be separable from bodies, with the sole exception of the universal soul from the universal body; for all bodies are in flux and perishable, except the one body of all, in its totality, which is eternal.

What then in respect of souls, he asks (vi.4.16), is the meaning of the popular phrase 'going to Hadēs' or 'being in Hadēs'?

Let Hadēs be taken to mean the Invisible. It is not the soul that goes anywhere; for it itself is not moved, but is rather the cause or principle of movement. But just as we say the soul is there, in that place where the body is, so when it is separated from the physical body, but has still attached to it the subtle image, it may be said to go to, or be in, what he calls the 'inferior place', where the impure spirit is.

---

[1] It was the Cambridge Platonist Dean Cudworth, in his *True Intellectual System of the Universe* (1st ed. 1678), who first in later years drew sympathetic attention to the theory of spirituous and celestial bodies according to these philosophers, and won the commendation of the learned world for his exposition. In 1733, however, J. L. Mosheim severely criticized Cudworth's exposition (see J. Harrison's translation of M.'s Latin notes, in the 1845 (London) edition of C.'s famous work, iii.299ff.). M. is never weary of inveighing against what he calls the 'insane imaginings' of the 'Junior Platonists', whom he stigmatises as 'superstitious, trifling, credulous and fanatical' (p. 307, n), chiefly because they worked what we now call primitive culture notions into their all-embracing system. But can any true philosophy of human experience omit what is so elemental and fundamental? This bad habit set by Mosheim has generally obtained in academic circles up to the present day.

Even in the case of a soul set free by philosophy from a separate body or embodiment of any kind, and so abiding in purity in the intelligible state, or spiritual world proper in the highest sense of the term, the image still persists for a certain time in Hadēs.

This is an ancient notion concerning the heroes, or daimonic souls, Plotinus thinks (i.1.12); for Homer (*Od.* xi.602-5) 'appears to admit this doctrine in the case of Hercules, speaking of his image as being in Hadēs, while he himself is among the Gods.'

The image, or *eidōlon*, is intimately connected with the irrational soul, which is poetically said to be the shadow cast by the shining of the rational soul on the body (i.1.2). The irrational soul is also said to be the image of the rational plunged into the obscurity of sensible life (iv.3.27).

Elsewhere (ii.2.2), speaking of a certain sphere-like or spherical psychical element, Plotinus avers that whereas the proper movement of life is circular, as is most clearly seen in the heavenly bodies, the movement of our physical bodies is rectilinear. But there is also a circular or sphere-like body in us. It has, however, become terrestrial or obscure, and is no longer light as in the case of heavenly bodies.

The nature of the movement of the spirit is probably of this kind. The spirit is the element that moves circle-wise in us. It is originally as it were an aëry or igneous body, the inner clothing or attachment of the soul before it descends into a terrestrial body (iv.3.9, 15).

This view of the meaning of 'going to Hadēs', or 'being in Hadēs', Porphyry also expounds in his summary of Plotinian doctrine.[1]

Thus he tells us that in the same way as 'being on earth' is for the soul, not its moving about on earth, as physical bodies do, but having control of a body that moves about on earth, so also 'being in Hadēs' for the soul is when it has attached to it the management of an image or spirit which has its existence in space, or whose nature it is to be in a place.

This image, in the case of the unpurified, is of a dark or cloudy nature. Accordingly, if Hadēs is the 'underworld', and therefore an obscure state of existence compared with the celestial spheres, the soul may be said to go there so long as it has such a darkened image attached to it.

By 'being in Hadēs' is then meant that the soul is in the state of its invisible and darkened 'nature' (*physis*).

It is owing to the propensity of the 'partial reason' of the soul towards such and such a body, owing to its habit, or its habitual relationship to a certain body on earth, that a certain form or type of phantasy or imaging is impressed upon the spirit

[1] *Sent. ad Intelligibilia ducentes*, xxix.; p. 13f. (ed. Mommert, Leipzig, 1907); P. is commenting on *En.* iv.3.9.

after death, the spirit itself having no special form.[1]

But what is the meaning of going 'beneath the earth', to the subterrene or under-world?[2]

Porphyry assumes that the impure spirit may be so heavy, or watery, as he calls it, that it can be said to go to the under-world. But he reiterates that the essence or life or consciousness of the soul itself cannot be said to change place or be in a place, but only that it contracts the habits of bodies whose nature is to change place and occupy space. For as is the disposition of the soul, so does it obtain a body conditioned in rank and properties. Just as the soul can be kept on earth only by means of the earthy shell, so can it be kept in Hadēs only by its attachment to the image or moist spirit.

According to ancient physics the downward ele-

[1] Cp. Porph. *Comm. in Odyss.* p. 130, 31 (ed. Schrader): 'For to souls, according to the poet [Homer], the images of their experiences above [? on earth] continue to appear as phantasms below as well'; *De Abstin.* p. 168, 7 (ed. Nauck); 'The shapes which characterize this spirit are moulded in many forms'; *Ad Gaur.* v.1: 'Daimones make the forms of the phantasms appear on the aëry spirit, whether this spirit be their own or that of someone else.' The daimones, or let us say 'spirits' in the spiritistic sense, it should be noted, may be good or bad; they are not necessarily bad like the demons of the Christians.

[2] It should be remembered that according to Orphic notions, which broke away from the primitive Babylonian, Semitic and Egyptian conceptions of Sheol and Amenti, the subterrene proper was believed to be the lower state of Tartarus. The higher regions of Hades were supposed to extend from the earth-surface to the moon. This improvement was owing to the influence of the doctrines of astral or sidereal religion.

ments are the earthy and moist (the moist being sup-posed originally to extend below the earth) and the upward the airy and fiery. The soul has thus the humid or moist element attached to it as long as it wills to associate with, or has its attention fixed on, things in generation.

The idea that the moist principle was that which conditioned all genesis, generation, or birth-and-death, that it, so to say, constituted the ocean of animal and plantal life, the state of perpetual flux, or ever-becoming, was a general dogma of the school. Indeed, it seems to have been a leading notion of ancient mystic lore in general.

Thus we find Porphyry elsewhere[1] explaining the Egyptian symbolism of the boats or barques of the 'daimones' as being intended to represent not solid bodies, but the vehicles in which they 'sail on the moist'.

This applied to all grades, from the soul of the sun-god to all souls that descend into genesis. And with regard to the latter Porphyry cites the *logoi* of Heraclitus: 'For souls to become moist is delight or death', delight consisting in their falling into genera-tion; and: 'We live their [the souls'] death, and they live our death.'[2]

---

[1] *De Ant. Nymph.* x., where he cites as his authority Numenius the Alexandrian Pythagoreo-Platonic philosopher and student of what we should now call comparative religion, who flourished in the middle of the 2nd century.

[2] Cp. Diels (2nd ed. Berlin, 1906), fr. 77; cp. fr. 36; 'For souls it

Elsewhere in the same treatise[1] Porphyry tells us that, according to the Stoics, souls who love the body attract a moist spirit to them, and condense it like a cloud (for the moist being condensed in air constitutes a cloud). That when the spirit in souls is condensed by a superabundance of the moist element, they become visible. Of such are the apparitions of images of the deceased that are occasionally met with; the spirit being furthermore coloured and shaped by phantasy, that is the imagination.

The rest of the Neoplatonic philosophers held more or less the same general views on the nature of the spirit-body in its unpurified state. There was, however, a great difference of opinion as to whether or not the soul could be entirely separated from this body. Some held that it could; others contended that it was only its impurities that could be cast off, as we shall see when we come to treat of what they called the luciform or radiant vehicle.

That there were many different views among the philosophical schools in general, not only on the more transcendental relationships of the soul, but also on the inferior connection between soul and body, may be seen from Philoponus (9, 35f.; 10, 4f.[2]), to whose

is death to become water', and fr. 62: 'Immortal mortals, mortal immortals, the one living the death and dying the life of the other.'

[1] De Ant. Nymph. xi., p. 64, ed. Nauck.

[2] The references are to Philoponi in Aristotelis de Anima, ed. M. Hayduck (Berlin, 1897), Comm. in. Arist. Graec. Acad. Litt. Reg. Ber. vol. xv. There is, unfortunately, no English translation.

instructive commentary on Aristotle's famous treatise *On the Soul* we may now turn. Philoponus was in an excellent position to review the whole ground; moreover he sought to reconcile, or make a 'symphony' of, Plato and Aristotle.

He contends (10, 4f.) that the true doctrine of these two great masters is (12, 15): that every soul is incorporeal; that whereas the rational soul alone is separable from every body, and on this account is not subject to death, the irrational is separable from the physical body, but inseparable from the spirit – that is, the spirituous body – which persists for a certain time after its departure from the gross body. As to the vegetative soul, it has its existence in the physical body only and perishes together with it. There is no spirit-body in plants (17, 8f.).

This last point is straitly contradicted by the long tradition of Alchemy which bestows 'spirits' not only on plants but also on metals. Philoponus later on admits a 'somewhat' of vegetative life in the animal spirit-body.

The irrational soul persists after death, having as its vehicle or substrate the spirituous body, which is composed of the four elements, but has in it a preponderance of air, just as the earthy body has a preponderance of earth (17, 20).[1]

The spirit-body is the medium of existence in

[1] This view differs somewhat from that of the Trismegistic school (see p. 37 above).

Hadēs, and also provides a basis for the phantasms of the deceased.

As to the chastisements in Hadēs, they cannot really purify the soul; for the soul being self-moved must purify itself of its own free-will, and must, therefore, return to earth for this purpose. The chastisements are simply for the purpose of turning it to itself, causing it to repent, or wean itself from sympathy with the things of generation (17, 25 – 18, 25).

As to the inferior means of purification and the *rationale* of phantasms of the deceased, Philoponus has the following (19, 24ff.):

'Now they say that the spirit-body also has somewhat of the vegetative life, for it also is nourished – not however in the same way as this [gross body], but by means of vapours, not by parts [i.e. by separate organs], but the whole of it through the whole [as one organism], so to say, just like a sponge. And so those who are in earnest favour a lighter and drier diet, to prevent its becoming dense.

'Moreover they say there are certain means of purification. As this [gross body] is cleansed with water, so is that [spirituous body] by purifications of vapours; for it is nourished with certain vapours and cleansed with others.[1]

'They say it is not provided with organs; but the

---

[1] The same reason is given for the use of the famous Egyptian incense *kuphi* by Plutarch, *De I. et O.*, lxxix.2, where he speaks of its 'fanning up [the fire of] the spirit connate with the body'.

whole of it, through the whole of it, is active as a sensory and lays hold of sensible objects.

'Wherefore also Aristotle says, in his *Metaphysics* [p. 455ᵃ, 20], that properly sense is one, and the true sensory one, by sensory meaning the spirit, in which the sense-power as a whole, through the whole [sensory], lays hold of the manifold objects of sense.'

But if it have no organs, how can it be said to account for phantasms which apparently have organs, and manifest sometimes in the forms of men and sometimes in other animal forms?

In the first place, when made dense with a heavy diet, it is readily 'moulded into the shape of its surrounding body, just as happens with ice, which takes the shape of the vessels in which it is formed.'

But this does not account for its taking *different* forms.

To this they say 'it is probable that, when the soul desires to manifest, it shapes itself [that is, the spirit-body], setting its own imagination in movement; or even that it is probable with the help of daimonic co-operation that it appears and again becomes invisible, being condensed and rarefied' – a theory that may not be without interest to modern spiritists and those familiar with the phenomena of 'materialising' *séances*; for here 'daimonic co-operation' might easily be rendered 'spirit-help'.

It is, moreover, laid down as a general dogma that the power of sensation resides not in the physical body but in the spirit (161, 4). It is, for instance, not the ear, nor even the membrane or drum of the ear, that is the hearing sensory,[1] but the spirit (353, 32).

In brief, it is the spirit-body that is the unitary or common sense-organ (433, 34).

This, Philiponus says, is the doctrine of both Aristotle and the Platonici. Thus he tells us (438, 25) that, according to Aristotle:

'The first sensory, in which is the sensing power, is the spirit, the substrate of the irrational soul; for in this the sense has first of all its being.

'Eyes, ears and nostrils are sense-organs only, they do not come first, for the feeling soul is not in them. They are the means whereby sensible experience is referred to the spirit.'

And again (239, 3), according to Aristotle:

'The powers of sensation are established in the spirit, for the whole, through the whole of it, both sees and hears and is active in the rest of the senses. And thus all the senses are in it, just as in plants are the vegetative powers.[2] . . . The spirit itself is not organized.'

The Platonists also declare, he tells us (597, 23),

---

[1] Cp. 364, 15; and for the 'visual spirit', 161, 25; 336, 17; 20, 33, 37; 337, 6, 14ff. It should be remembered that ancient physiology was apparently totally ignorant of the nervous system. The problem for us to-day is removed a stage; it is, however, fundamentally the same problem.

[2] Cp. 201, 31: 'In the spirit, however, the psychic powers are disposed, as are the vegetative in trees, the whole of them being spread throughout the whole spirit.'

that 'the apprehension of sensibles does not at all take place through the [physical organs], inasmuch as both in us [i.e. in the case of men] the common sense, residing in a single spirit, perceives the objects of the five senses, and the irrational soul [in the case of animals] by means of a single spirit apprehends all sensibles.'

And so in general Philoponus sums up the doctrine as follows (481, 19ff.):

'The common sense, which in itself is incorporeal, functions in the body which is its ground. This ground is the spirituous body. Thus the various orders of sensible phenomena, though different from one another, occur in the spirituous body, now in one portion, now in another of it. Subsequently the power itself [i.e. the common sense] discriminates the sensible experiences in the spirit. And so we keep the reason free [from sense], and do not say that different forms occur in that which has no parts [*sc.* the rational soul], but [that they occur] in the greatest [body], that is the spirituous, in different portions of it.'

The spirit-body being thus regarded as the true sensory, it was also thought to be the medium for what are now called thought-transference and telepathy, for 'inner voices' also, both bad and good. And so, we find Psellus, in his famous treatise on the daimones – here meaning non-human as well as human discarnate entities – (p. 94 [p. 72]) suggesting that the way the lower orders of these invisibles insinuate their temptations into men's souls, is by immediately affecting the phantastic spirit or imaginal essence:

'When a man addresses another from a distance he has to speak more loudly, but if he be close, he can whisper into his ear.

'If, moreover, it were possible for him to come into close contact with the spirit of his soul, he would need no uttered speech, but all he wanted to say would reach the hearer by a soundless way.

'They say that this is also the way with souls on leaving the body; for they, too, communicate with one another without sound.'

It need hardly be pointed out that this more immediate communication of mind with mind is a common persuasion, from the days of Swedenborg to the present, in all the modern rumours of the hither hereafter.

Not only delirium, Philoponus tells us (164), but also the frequent derangement and dulling of the understanding when a man is not in possession of his normal senses, are supposed to be due to changes in this spirit, when, according to Aristotle (418^b, 24), 'the spirituous body either undergoes a certain breakdown or, by being out of symmetry, troubles and hampers the understanding.'

So also with regard to memory, Philoponus explains (158, 7) that, though the memory-movement may be said to start from the soul, 'we do not mean that the soul remembers of itself by itself; but that, just as in the case of the senses we say that the movement starting from the sensible objects reaches that in which the discriminating and perceptive power [resides] – namely, the spirit – so also in the case of memory we say that it is from the spirit in which the soul is [vehicled], that the start of the memory-movement takes place.'

That academic psychology will deign seriously to consider the hypothesis of the 'spirit-body' in any shape or form does not seem as yet very probable. Psychical research, however, appears with every day to be more and more driven in this direction.

Of course the vastly greater knowledge of physiology and biology which we now possess must very considerably change the ancient doctrine in many respects; but the main notion in its simplest form has so well fitted in with the unsophisticated experience of mankind for so many ages, that it may still be found in some respects to deserve the scrutiny of unprejudiced investigation.

The Radiant Body

Though the term 'Augoeides' has been popularised by Bulwer Lytton, the majority of readers of the novelist know no more about the mystical doctrine concerning it than they may have gleaned from the somewhat confused 'Soliloquy of Zanoni':

'Soul of mine, the luminous, the Augoeides, why descendest thou from thy sphere – why from the eternal, star-like and passionless serene, shrinkest thou back to the mists, the dark sarcophagus? How long, too austerely taught that companionship with the things that die brings with it but sorrow in its sweetness, hast thou dwelt contented with thy majestic solitude!'[1]

To this the author, in the 1853 edition, appended a note, containing a paragraph in Greek, to which the reference and of which the translation are both erroneous. The passage is from Marcus Aurelius (xi.12), and runs as follows:

'The sphere of the soul is radiant (*augoeidēs*)[2]

[1] *Zanoni*, bk. ii, ch. 4 (1st ed., 1845). *Zanoni* was developed from a crude and floridly romantic sketch called 'Zicci,' a serial contributed to *The Monthly Chronicle*, in 1838. The 'soliloquy' is not found in 'Zicci,' ch. iv.

[2] This is a questionable reading, though it may have some probability from the concluding paragraph of the context; the latest texts read *autoeidēs*, that is 'like itself, uniform, self-formed'. (See

when it is neither extended to any [object], nor is contracted inwards, nor is convoluted,[1] nor collapses, but when it is made to shine with [that] light whereby it sees the truth – the [truth] of all things, and the [truth] in itself.'

Let us then see whether, with a modicum of industry, a little more light may be thrown on the subject.

In classical Greek, *augoeidēs* is an adjective meaning 'possessed of a form of *augē*' – that is, of a form of splendour, brightness, brilliance, radiance; hence brilliant, shining, radiant, ray-like, luciform, glorious, etc.

So much for the dictionary. But what of the *augoeides* as the radiant body, or glorious vehicle or vesture of the soul?

We have already discussed at some length the ideas of the Later Platonists, and of their immediate predecessors and successors, on the nature of the spirituous vehicle, or spirit-body, or spirit (*tò pneûma* or *tò sôma pneumatikón*), and may therefore proceed, without further introduction, to treat of that prime essence or substance of all bodies, and of all embodiment, to which these philosophers most commonly give the name *augoeides*.

D. *Imp. M. Ant. Com. Libri XXII.*, rec. I. Stich, Leipzig, 1903, p. 147.)

[1] Reading σπειρᾶται for σπείρηται; this gives the idea of coil, spiral or convolution, of ovoid as compared with perfect sphere.

The root-notion was most probably taken over into Greek philosophy from Orphism – that is to say, presumably from the influence of the Old Oriental mystic doctrines of Asia Minor or Hither Asia on Hellenic thought.

Now the line of descent for their 'theology' was traced by the Platonici themselves from Orpheus to Pythagoras and Plato.

Let us then, first, turn to the earliest and latest of the School of the Academy – to Plato himself and to Damascius – and hear what they have to say about this sensible vehicle of purity and truth.

In that magnificent passage of the *Phaedrus* (250c) in which he speaks of the Vision of Heavenly Beauty, Plato dwells on the philosophic memory or reminiscence of that state when the souls of men had not yet fallen into generation, and continues:

'There was a time when they could behold Beauty in all its brilliance, when, together with the rest of the Blessed Company – we [philosophers] in the train of Zeus, and other [ranks of souls] in the train of some other of the Gods – they both beheld the beatific spectacle and [divine] vision, and were initiated into that mystery, which truly may be called the holiest of all, in which we joyed in mystic ecstasy.

'For then we were ourselves still in the state of wholeness and unconscious of the evils that awaited us in time to come – not only being made mystically conscious of[1] the [divine] forms,[2] in wholeness yet in singleness, void of all motion yet filled full of bliss; but also eye to eye beholding[3] them in radiance (*augē*) of purity.

'For we were [then] pure [ourselves] and not yet sunk into this "tomb" (*sēma*), which now we bear about with us and call it "body" (*sōma*), bound fast [to it] like oyster [to its shell].'[4]

To pass from the grandiose intuition of the Founder of the school to the last occupant of the *kathédra* of the Academy, Damascius, who was driven from the Chair in 529 by Justinian. In his Commentary (§414) on the *Parmenidēs* of Plato, Damascius writes of the radiant vehicle as follows:

'In heaven, indeed, our radiant (*augoeidés*) [portion] is full filled with heavenly radiance (*augē*) – a glory that streams throughout its depths, and lends it a divine strength.

'But in lower states, losing this [radiance], it is dirtied, as it were, and becomes darker and darker and more material.

'Heedless it grows, and sinks down towards the

---

[1] μυούμενοι – indicating the lower grade of the *myēsis*, with eyes shut or veiled.

[2] *Phásmata, sc.* the Ideas.

[3] ἐποπτεύοντες – signifying the higher degree of the *epopteía*, with eyes open or unveiled.

[4] Jowett's translation (i.456) misses almost every one of the technical points. Shall we say this is owing to his over-anxiety to 'modernize' Plato for literary purposes?

earth; yet in its essence is it still the same in number [i.e. a unity].

'So also with our soul itself, when it strives upwards unto Mind and God, then is its essence [sc. the augoeides] full filled with gnostic light divine, of which it previously [sc. in incarnation] was not possessed, else had it always been divine.'[1]

Damascius also says elsewhere[2] that Isidōrus, who was the friend of Proclus and Marinus, and husband of Hypatia, and who occupied the *kathédra* of the school for a brief period, had stated, on the authority of some other philosopher, whom we can no longer identify owing to the loss of the context, that:

'The soul has a certain radiant vehicle (*augoeidès óchēma*), as it is called,[3] starlike (*astroeidés*) and eternal. And this [vehicle] is securely shut away in this [gross] body, according to some within the head, [and] according to others within the right shoulder – a statement which no one else seems to have made.'

It is doubtful whether the last clause is due to Damascius or to Suidas. In any case it refers solely

---

[1] Ruelle (C. A.), *Damascii Successoris Dubitationes et Solutiones de Primis Principiis in Platonis Parmenidem* (Paris, 1889), ii.270. There is a French translation by A. E. Chaignet (Paris, 1908, 3 vols.); cp. iii.147.

[2] In his *Life of Isidorus*, which is lost. We owe the quotation to the *Lexicon* of Suidas, ed. Bernhardy (Halle, 1853), 1, 850f.; ed. Bekker (Berlin, 1854), p. 194.

[3] As, for instance, in the Chaldaean Oracles' poem, 'the subtle vehicle (*leptòn ochēma*) of the soul', quoted by Hierocles in his commentary on *The Golden Verses* of Pythagoras, xxvi. 67-69.

to the queer statement about the 'right shoulder.'

Perhaps it is then hardly worth while in this connection to remind ourselves of a certain mystic 'silver cord,'[1] or psychical attachment, which is variously 'seen' and spoken of. This is supposed by a few figuratively to start from between the shoulder-blades; it is also imagined to unroll itself as it were from a point or centre, and contract itself again into a point, when the subtle vehicle leaves and returns to the body in certain mystic experiences. The phenomenon is very variously described, and the cord has numerous points of attachment according to others.

The *augoeides* was, however, as we see, thought more usually to be centred, as it were a light-spark, in the head – that is, its only point of contact with the physical body was imagined to be in the head – whereas the spirituous body, as we have seen in our last essay, was thought of as pervading the whole gross body and surrounding it.

We may now turn to two passages of a more detailed nature, taken from the works of Porphyry (†A.D. 305) and of Proclus (†A.D. 485). In his *Sententiæ*, which are practically a summary of Plotinian doctrine, speaking of the soul, Porphyry tells us that:

'When it is in a purer condition, it has cognate

---

[1] The reference to a 'silver cord' will indubitably remind the reader of the phrase in the magnificent, but exceedingly puzzling, concluding outburst of Koheleth (*Eccl.* xii.6). But the treatment of the whole passage, xii.1-8, would be too long a story for this occasion.

with it the body that is nighest to the immaterial [state] – viz. the aethereal (*aithérion*) body.

'But when it proceeds from reason (*lógos*) into the projection of imagination (*phantasia*), it has cognate with it the sunlike (*hēlioeidés*) [body].

'When further it becomes womanish and grows impassioned for form, it has the moonlike (*selēnoeidés*) [body] present with it.

'And [finally] when it falls into bodies – [which it does] whenever it gets into an amorphous state – composed of moist exhalations, complete ignorance of reality, obscuration and childishness supervene for it . . .

'When, however, it tries to separate itself from [this] nature, it becomes a dry radiance (*augē*) shadowless and cloudless.

'For moisture forms cloud in air,[1] while dryness changes vapour into dry radiance (*augē*).[2]

With this we may compare the following passage from Proclus' Commentary on the *Timaeus* of Plato:

'Man is a little world (*mikrós kósmos*). For, just like the universe (*tò pân*), he possesses both mind and reason (*noûs* and *lógos*), both a divine and mortal body. He is also divided up according to the universe.

'It is for this reason, you know, that some are accustomed to say that his gnostic [principle] (*tò*

[1] Cp. Porph. *De Ant. Nymp.* p. 64, 16 (Nauck): 'For moisture in air being densified produces cloud.'

[2] Porphyrii, *Sententiae ad Intelligibilia Ducentes*, xxix.; p. 14f., ed. Mommert (Leipzig, 1907).

noeròn) corresponds with the nature of the fixed stars,

'His reason [corresponds] in its contemplative aspect with Saturn, and in its social aspect with Jupiter.

'As to his irrational [part] – the passional [nature corresponds] with Mars, the eloquent with Mercury, the appetitive with Venus, the sensitive with Sol, and the vegetative with Luna.

'Moreover, the radiant vehicle (*augoeidès óchēma*) [corresponds] with heaven, and this mortal [frame] with the sublunary [region].'[1]

In these two passages we have two different schemes of ordering the psychical embodiment and activities of man, the lesser world, in correspondence with the astral components of the greater world.

Porphyry follows the ancient ordering of old Babylonian tradition, where the Sun and Moon succeed to the pure ethereal space and precede the 'planets'. Proclus uses the languge of the later Neo-Babylonian astrologers, and that too in a Hellenized or philosophized form.

Now the general tenor of the most recent research justifies us in ascribing the introduction of the idea of the *augoeides* into Greek religio-philosophy to ancient Orphic mystagogy blended with Pythagoreanism. Indeed, as is well known and as we have said before, the Platonici themselves invariably claimed that the sources of their 'theology' went back

[1] Procli, *Commentarius in Platonis Timaeum*, p. 384A, B, ed. Schneider (Vratislaviae, 1847), p. 848.

through Plato and Pythagoras to Orpheus himself.

It is, therefore, of interest to see what Hierocles, the Neoplatonic philosopher of Alexandria, who flourished in the middle of the fifth century, has to tell us of this radiant body, in his Commentary on *The Golden Verses*, which contained the so-called 'symbols' of the Pythagorean discipline.

These 'symbols' are enigmatic sayings or allegorical precepts envisaging moral truths. They are technically known as *akoúsmata* or 'things heard'. The most recent opinion, that of Professor Burnet, will have it that most of them are 'tabus of a thoroughly primitive type'.[1]

Hierocles tells us practically that the object of the whole of the purificatory degrees of this far-famed method of discipline was nothing else than the restoration of this quintessential embodiment to its original state.

'The end of the method of the Pythagoreans was that they should become furnished with wings [to soar] to the reception of the divine blessings, in order that, when the day of death comes, the Athletes in the Games of Philosophy [i.e. of the Love of Wisdom], leaving the mortal body on earth, and stripping off its nature [*sc.* the spirituous body], may be unencumbered for the heavenly journey.'[2]

---

[1] See art. 'Pythagoras and Pythagoreanism', in the last published volume of Hastings' *Encyclopaedia of Religion and Ethics*.

[2] Ed. Needham (Cambridge, 1709), p. 227.

And so also, commenting, in § xxvi., on verses 67-69, he tells us:

'From these verses, whoever of us is not inattentive to the Pythagorean counsels, should learn that, together with the discipline (*askēsis*) of virtue and the recovery of truth, he shall also be diligent in the purification of his radiant (*augoeidés*) body, which the [Chaldaean] Oracles also call the subtle vehicle of the soul.'[1]

And this he repeats a little later as follows:

'Just as, then, it is necessary to adorn (*kosmesai*) the soul with science (*epistēmē*) and virtue, so that it may be able to company with those who are eternally wise and virtuous, so also must we make our radiant (*augoeidés*) [body] pure and free from [gross] matter, in order that it may support communion with the aethereal bodies.'[2]

From the above passages, we may be permitted to deduce that the chief grades of this spiritual discipline were: purity, virtue and truth.

We may now conclude this part of our essay by some apposite quotations from Philoponus, who lived at Alexandria in the first half of the seventh century, and who was, as we saw in our last sketch, in a very favourable position to sum up the doctrines of the Platonic school. The chief passage of Philoponus on the *augoeides* runs as follows:

[1] Needham, p. 214; Mullach (Paris, 1860), p. 478b.
[2] *Sc.* the stars and bodies of the Gods; Needham, p. 222, Mullach, p. 481b.

'There is, moreover, beyond this [spirituous body] another kind of body, that is for ever attached to [the soul], of a celestial nature, and for this reason ever-lasting, which they call radiant (*augoeidés*) or star-like (*astroeidés*).

'For as [the soul] is a being of the cosmic order, it is absolutely necessary that it should have an estate or portion of the cosmos in which to keep house.

'And if [the soul] is in a state of perpetual motion, and it is necessary that it should be for ever in activity it needs must be that it should ever have attached [to it] some body or other which it keeps eternally alive.

'For these reasons, therefore, they say it for ever keeps its radiant (*augoeidés*) [body], which is of an everlasting nature.'[1]

Speaking of this heavenly 'body' from the macro-cosmic standpoint, Philoponus tells us that, accord-ing to the Platonici, 'the matter of celestial [bodies]' is not of the four elements, but 'there is another kind of body – the fifth', element, or quintessence, and its form (*eídos*) is spherical.[2]

Afterwards, in treating of it from the microcosmic point of view, he writes:

'Further, it is necessary to show that the rational soul has the essence [or substance, *ousía*] of every body attached to it; while the other [souls] have

[1] *Philoponi in Aristotelis de Anima*, ed. Hayduck (Berlin, 1897), 18, 26ff.
[2] *Ib.* 56, 3; cp. 88, 12; 138, 6; 21, 22, and also 450, 29, where it is called the 'aethereal', and the four others the 'single bodies'.

their existence in a [certain order of] body – viz. the irrational [soul] in the spirit [or spirituous body] and the vegetative in this [gross body]' (15, 19).

Finally, in commenting on Aristotle's *De An.* ii.7, Philoponus tells us that, according to Aristotle:

'The everlasting, the sublime (*ánō*) body, partakes of transparency; and he calls it the out-flow (*chúma*) of the spheres, for all [of them] are transparent' (324, 5).[1] It pertains to the 'crystalline'.

Though the dogma of the inseparability of the soul from its essential substance or vehicle (the *augoeides*) was the general belief of the Platonic school – for without the latter, as they contended,[2] the soul could not continue in activity or actuality – there was also a purely absolutist doctrine of complete separability, which Aristotle tried to saddle on the master himself, as a deduction from a statement in the *Timaeus*.

This is set forth by Philoponus as follows:

'Now in Plato's view it is better for the soul to be without body [of any kind]. For life in body is full of toil for it.

'He believed, moreover, that the cosmos will never be dissolved. And so the soul of the universe will be in a less fortunate state than, and not on an equality with, our souls; inasmuch as *they* will at some time be

---

[1] This is the 'astral' light-body notion. Some think that the name 'Al-chymy,' is derived from *chyma*, the *al* being of course the Arabic definite article. Alchemy first reappeared in the West through Latin translations from the Arabic versions of Greek originals.

[2] See the first quotation from P. (18, 26f.) above.

freed from their body. Whereas the [universal] soul has to be forever inwoven with the [universal] body.

'At any rate Aristotle finely draws this conclusion, if really, as the *Timaeus* seems to say, the essence of the [world-] soul is inwoven with the [world-] body.

'But [on the contrary] even as the [human] soul, when it gains the mastery over the [physical] body, has this body following it, and does not itself follow the motions of the body, so, *à fortiori*, when the celestial body [of the universe] is free from all mortal disturbance and is moved solely by the will of the [world-] soul, no disturbance results to the soul from it.

'And this is also the case with our own soul and its radiant (*augoeidés*) [body]' (137, 27ff.).

The rest of this quest will be devoted to the consideration of what Synesius has to tell us about the *augoeides*.

Synesius (A.D. 365-430?) was a Neo-platonist and for many years a correspondent of Hypatia's. Indeed he sent his treatise *On Visions*, from which the following quotations are taken, to 'the philosopher' for her approval.

This treatise was written about A.D. 404, before Synesius became a Christian. He subsequently, about twenty-three years after, held a bishopric for some three years before his death.

As what Synesius has to tell us is the most detailed statement on the subject known to me, I venture to append a careful and full translation which may be all the more acceptable as there exists no English version.[1]

'7 (135D). If to see God with one's eyes [in sensible nature] is a felicitous experience, the comprehension [of Him] by means of imagination (*phantasía*) pertains to a higher order of intuition.

'For this [power of imagination] is the [one] sense of [all differentiated] senses, seeing that the spirit (*pneûma*), whereby the imagination is brought into play, is the most general sensory and the first body of the soul.

'It has its seat in the innermost place, and dominates the living creature (136A) as it were from a citadel. For round it nature has built up the whole economy of the head.

'Now hearing and sight are not senses, but organs of sense, servants of the common [sense], as it were door-keepers, who notify their mistress of the sense-objects outside, whereby the out-turned organs of sense have their doors knocked upon.

[1] The only version with which I was acquainted when I made the following translation, in 1910, was the utterly valueless rendering, or rather paraphrase, of H. Druon (Paris, 1878), which consistently misses every characteristic point. I was then under the impression that nothing in the way of a rendering existed in English, but subsequently came across W. S. Crawford's condensed summary, pp. 473ff., in his instructive volume *Synesius the Hellene* (London, 1901). It is, however, in no way a translation and a very imperfect guide as a summary. The text used is I. G. Krabinger's edition of the Homilies and Fragments (Landshut, 1850), pp. 323ff.

'Whereas she in all portions of her is simple sense. For she hears with the whole of the spirit [*sc.* the common sensory], and sees with the whole of it; and so she does for the rest of the senses.

'She it is who distributes the powers [of sense] among the various [sense] organs. And they each proceed from the animal [i.e. the spirit]; and are, as it were, kinds of radii, issuing from a centre and centring into it, being all one in respect of their common root, but many in their procession.

'Accordingly sense, when proceeding through the projected organs, is of a most animal-like nature. Indeed it is not sense at all before it arrives at its source. The immediate sense is more divine and closer to the soul.

'And so let no one whose imaginative spirit (*phantastikòn pneûma*) is diseased, expect clear and unconfused visions.

'Now what its disease is, both by what things it is made blear-eyed and dense, and by what it is cleansed and purged and returns to its natural state, you must learn from the mystic philosophy,[1] whereby also, after it has been purified by perfecting rites (*teletôn*), it becomes God-possessed.

'Before, however, the [body of] imagination can receive God, the incomings [of sense must] flee away out of it.

'But he who keeps it pure, by living a life accord-

[1] *Sc.* The Chaldaean Oracles.

ing to nature, has it ever in readiness, to be the most extended common-sensory [even] in this life.

'Spirit so purified is sensible of the dispositions of the soul, and is not unsympathetic in itself [to them], as is the shell-like envelope [sc. the gross body]. (137A.)

'The latter indeed has ever an antagonistic nature to the higher dispositions of the soul; whereas its primal and eternal vehicle is subtilised and aetherealised when [the soul] is made virtuous. But when it is made vicious, its vehicle becomes dense and earthy.

'For this spirit is precisely the border-land between unreason and reason, between body and the bodiless. It is the common frontier of both, and by its means things divine are joined with lowest things.

'Therefore it is difficult for its nature to be comprehended by philosophy [alone].[1]

'8 (137B). For it lays under contribution what suits it, from both of the extremes, as from neighbours, and images in one single nature things that are poles apart.

'As to the extent of this imaginative essence, nature has poured it into many divisions of being. Indeed it goes down even as low as irrational creatures, so as the better to extend itself.

'Moreover the whole of the genera of daimones are supplied with their substance by this mode of life

[1] Sc. philosophy as distinguished from 'mystic philosophy'.

[or animal]. For during the whole of their existence they are of the nature of images and take on the appearances of happenings.[1]

'As for man he is conscious of many things by means of this [essence] even when by itself, and of more when there is another [? a daimōn or spirit] with it.

'For [the orders of daimones] make thoughts always to have some mixture of imagination, except perchance a man in a flash establish immaterial contact with an idea.

'But the transcending of imagination is as difficult as it is blissful.

'For "mind and wisdom", says [Plato, *Phileb.* 59D], are beloved by him to whomsoever they come even in 'old age', meaning [by this] the power that transcends imagination.

'For the life that is pictured forth is surely of the imagination or of a mind that has recourse to imagination.

'9 (137D). In any case this psychic spirit, which the blessed ones[2] call also "spirituous soul", becomes both a god, and a daimōn capable of assuming any

[1] This is a remarkable and highly suggestive statement, and might well be used as a working hypothesis by those engaged in modern psychical research.

[2] Referring to the 'initiated' of the tradition preserved in the Hellenistic poem known as the Chaldæan Oracles. The *scholium* of Nicephorus (N. Gregoriae *Byzantinae Historiae Libri XXXVII.*, Migne, *Pat. Gr.*, tom. cxlix., col. 569) erroneously glosses it as 'the sacred writers among the Egyptians'.

form, and an image [or shade], in which last the soul works out its corrections.

'For not only the Oracles are in agreement about it, likening the manner of life of the soul in the after-state [of correction] to the image-happenings in dream, but also philosophy concludes that the first lives [on earth] are preparations for the second [in the after-state].

'It is, moreover, the higher habit of mind in souls which lightens [the spirit] and wipes off the stains of the lower [habit].

'(138A). And so by natural impulses it either rises on high owing to its heat and dryness – and this of course is [Plato's[1]] "winging" of the soul; moreover we find that Heracleitus's "wise soul, dry radiance (augē)"[2] comes to precisely the same thing.

'Or, becoming dense and moist, it sinks into the depths of earth by natural tendency, lurking [there], nay, thrust down into the subterrene state.[3]

'For this region is very suitable for moist spirits.

'Life in this state is miserable and penal. Yet it is possible even [for such a spirit], when it has been purified by time and toil and other lives, to rise. For, becoming a thing of double life, it runs a double course, and companies partly with the lower, and partly with the higher [regions].

'It is this [spirit] which the first soul, when it

---

[1] *Phaedr* 246D.   [2] Fr.118, Diels (Berlin, 1906).
[3] Cp. *Phaedo* 81C.

descends, has loaned to it from the spheres, and going on board of it, as on a boat, it comes into contact with the corporeal world.

'Thereon ensues a struggle, either to take it [the spirit] aloft with it, or it may be even no longer to continue with it. The latter, however, is a rare case.

'Nevertheless it may be compelled to let it go, if it will not follow. For it is not lawful to be unfaithful when once the initiatory rites have been known.

'It would indeed be a [sad] disgrace for souls to return [on high] without repaying what does not belong to them – leaving behind in the surround of the earth [instead of in the higher spheres] what they have borrowed on their way down.

'Yet even this may happen in the case of one or two as a grace of perfect initiation (*teletē*), yea of God.

'But the natural state [of affairs] is that, when the soul is once engrafted into [the spirit], they either pull together, or one pulls over or is pulled over by the other.

'But in any case they are joined together until the return [of the soul] to the state whence it came.

'And so when [the spirit] is weighed down by vice, it drags down together with it that soul who allows it to be so weighed down.

'And this is the warning that the Oracles give to the gnostic seed in us:

' "See that thou verge not down into the world of the dark rays; 'neath which is ever spread the abyss, devoid of form, where is no light to see, wrapped in black gloom, befouling, that joys in images (*eidōla*), void of all understanding."[1]

'For how can an infatuate life void of all understanding be a good thing for the mind? Whereas for the image this lower region is suitable, owing to the composition of its spirit being then of a similar nature. For 'like loves like'.[2]

'10 (138D). If, however, from their coupling, the two should become one, then the mind as well would be dowsed in the delight of pleasure.

'And, indeed, this would be the most extreme of ills – not to be conscious of the presence of evil. For this is the condition of those who no longer even try to rise – (139A) just like a hardened tumour, which gives no pain, nor reminds to seek a cure.

'And for this reason repentance (*metánoia*)[3] is an elevating means. For he who feels impatience with the circumstances in which he finds himself, devises means of escape.

'Now the chief thing in purification is the will. For then both deeds and words lend a helping hand. But when the will is absent, the whole purificatory dis-

---

[1] Using Kroll's text, p. 61; cp. my *Chaldaean Oracles* (London, 1908), ii.86.

[2] A Platonic proverb; cp. *Symp.* 195B, *Lys.* 214B, *Georg.* 510B.

[3] By this, as we see in the sequel, the philosophers meant a change of will, the conversion of the whole man.

cipline of initiation is soulless, being lopped of its chief characteristic.

'And on this account, both in this life and in the after-life, accesses [of suffering] afford the greatest and best service to the orders of existence, introducing pain and purging the soul of infatuate joy.

'And [so] what are mistakenly called misfortunes contribute largely to breaking up the habit we have for things here.

'Nay, the Divine Providence is revealed to those possessed of Mind by these [very happenings], which cause people who are not possessed [of Mind] to disbelieve in it; since it is not possible for the soul ever to turn its face away from matter if it does not come into collision with any evil in things here.

'Wherefore we should consider the successes that people talk so much about as a trap laid for souls by the overseers of things below.

'And so I leave to others the pretension that there may be a draught of oblivion [for souls] on their departure [from the physical body].

'It is rather when the soul enters into this life that an oblivion-draught is given it – the sweet and dulling drink down here.

'For, descending into its first life as a free worker, instead of so working, it volunteers for slavery.

'That is to say, it had to discharge a certain service to the nature of the world, according to the laws imposed by Destiny (*Adrásteia*).

'But, being bewitched by the gifts of matter, its condition resembles that of freemen who have hired themselves out by agreement for a time – who under the spell of some [slave] wench's beauty volunteer to stop, agreeing to serve the beloved object's master.

'And so do we, whenever we transfer our affections from the depth of the Mind to the state of bodily concerns and external so-seeming goods – so do we seem to agree with matter that it is fair.

'But she [sc. nature, matter's mistress] holds our agreement as a mystic secret bond; and even if we decide to be off as though freemen, she claims we are fugitives, and tries to bring us back again, and has us seized as runaways, quoting her document against [us].

'Then, indeed, is it that the soul has need of all its strength – yea, even of God – to help it. (140A). For it is no light business to put in a plea for the invalidation of one's own agreement, much less to obtain it by force.

'For then, indeed, by the decree of Fate, the avenging powers of matter are set in motion against those who take the bit in their teeth against nature's laws.

'And these, in truth, are the so-called trials, which the sacred stories (*hieroì lógoi*) say Hercules underwent and any other hero who valiantly strives for freedom, until they succeed in raising up their spirit to a height where the hands of nature cannot reach it.

'But if the leap is made within her borders, [the

spirit] is dragged down, and there is need of [still] more grievous struggles. For she is merciless, since the property already belongs to another [than ourselves]. Moreover, if [the soul] abandon the ascent in despair, she demands penalties for the attempt.

'11 (140B). In general, all lives are in error if [the soul] does not return along its first path.

'And see how vast a middle state this spirit has in which to play the part of citizen!

'Now if [the soul] verge downward,[1] the [sacred] utterance (*lógos*)[2] tells us, that [the spirit] is weighed down and sinks, until it light upon the "black-rayed gloom-wrapped" land.

'But if [the soul] strive upward, [the spirit] also follows with it, as far as ever it has the power to do so.

'This it can do until it comes to the furthest limit of the region opposite [*sc.* to the abyss]. Hear what the Oracles say also on this point:

' "Thou shalt leave no dross of matter in the height.
"The image also hath a portion in the light-wrapped land."[3]

'The "light-wrapped" is the antithesis of the "gloom-wrapped" region. With sharp eyes, moreover, we might see even something more in these words.

'For it is not seemly [for the soul] to restore to the

---

[1] Cp. Plat. *Phaedr.* 247B.   [2] *Sc.* the Oracle quoted above.
[3] Kroll, p. 61; see the writer's *Chaldaean Oracles*, ii. 81 and 38.

spheres the nature [*sc.* the spirit] which descended thence, without any addition. But whatever of the purest strata of both fire and air it drew into the image-nature in its descent, before it was enveloped in the earthy shell – this also, [the Oracle] says, it restores with it to the better "portion".

'Moreover it is reasonable that things which share in a common nature and are counted as one, should not be altogether without relation to one another, and especially things that have a neighbouring terri-tory – as, for instance, fire follows next on the circle-body [*sc.* the aether-sphere], and not as earth the last of existing things.

'And if the higher [elements] by yielding to the lower get some enjoyment out of the intercourse, and eventuate as a body of un-adulterated mud,[1] as though [the former] had been assimilated by that which was permitted to dominate in the conjunction, perhaps the lower [elements] as well, if they no longer struggle against the activity of the soul, but obey the reins and become submissive – by keeping step with it, and allowing the middle nature to follow the guidance of the first without pulling in every direction – may become aetherealized and restored [on high] together with it. At any rate, if not to the whole [height], they may pass beyond the highest point of the [four lower] elements, and experience the "light-wrapped" land. For [the Oracle] says,

[1] 'Mud' = water and earth, as opposed to air and fire above.

"it has a portion in it" – that is, in some order of the circling [aether].

'As to the part that comes from the elements, enough has been said, and we can believe it or disbelieve [as we choose].

'But as to the corporeal essence that comes thence [*sc.* from the aetheric spheres], it is quite impossible in nature that, when the soul returns above [this essence] should not arise from the corpse, and rising together with [the soul], be made accordant with the spheres, that is to say, be refunded as it were into its proper nature.

'12 (141c). Accordingly these two allotments – the "light-wrapped" and the "gloom-wrapped" – are the extremes, having as their portions the heights [and depths] of bliss and misery.

'And how many regions between, think you, [are there] in the main body (*kutos*) of the world, partly light and partly dark, in all of which the soul together with this spirit may live, changing its forms, and habits and lives?

'And so if [the soul] returns to its native nobility, it is a store-house of truth. For it is pure and transparent and immaculate, god and prophet, if it so will.

'But if it fall down, it becomes misty, and grows indefinite, and is false. For the mist-like [part] of the spirit cannot contain the activities of [all] the orders of existence, But being between [the two extremes], it misses some and hits others.

'You might thus judge of the daimonic nature also in any of its grades. (142A). For to speak truth absolutely or all but truth is characteristic of the divine or all but divine; whereas deception in prediction is ceaseless on the part of those who grovel towards matter – [deception] a thing of passion and of vain glory.

'For it is always by means of this [daimonic nature] that the lineage [of the soul] takes on the nature both of god and of major daimōn, and leaps up into and takes possession of the land made ready for the higher nature.'

What the nature of the radiant body was, in the beliefs of the Later Platonic school, has now been made sufficiently clear, I hope, from the above quotations. There may be other pertinent passages with which at present I am unacquainted, for the literature is extensive. But enough to have been adduced, I venture to think, to bring out clearly the main conception.

We pass now from what the philosophers thought to what Christians have taught on the subject. There were philosophers also among the Christians whose lamps may still be found to throw light on what otherwise must remain in the obscurity of miracle and dogma.

The Resurrection-Body

'I believe in . . . the resurrection of the flesh.' So runs the general creed of Christendom.

In the Eastern symbol this appears as: 'I look for the resurrection of the dead.' The Western 'Quicunque' affirms: 'All men shall rise again with their bodies. . . . This is the catholic faith.'[1]

The intention of the first and third declarations – in the popularly called Apostles' creed and Athanasian creed respectively – is plain enough: the resurrection-body is to be the restored physical body. The Nicene symbol is less explicit; it contents itself with the hope of resurrection only, without further definition.

On the nature of the happening hoped for in this fundamental belief of the Christian faith, there has been, since the earliest times, the greatest difference of opinion.

Omitting for the moment all reference to the views

---

[1] Both the Old Latin form (fourth century) and the Received form (eighth century) of the Apostles' creed have 'flesh' (*carnis, sarkós*); the Aquileian form (Rufinus, A.D. 390) and the form of St. Nicetas (A.D. 450) have 'of *this* flesh' (*hujus carnis*). The Nicaeno-Constantinopolitan symbol, in the Received form of the Eastern Church, dating from A.D. 381, has 'resurrection of the dead' (*anástasin nekrôn*) but the original Acta of the Nicene Council omit this clause altogether. The Symbolum Quicunque reads 'together with their bodies' (*cum corporibus suis*).

of the first two centuries, the best known advocate of the absolute physical identity theory is the Latin Father Tertullian.

Writing in the earliest years of the third century, this great controversialist, lawyer and formalist triumphantly concludes his treatise *On the Resurrection of the Flesh* with the most positive declaration possible that the flesh, that is the physical body, shall rise again in the case of every one – the very same flesh in its absolute identity and in its absolute integrity.[1] The frankly materialistic view could hardly be stated more categorically.

In subsequent controversies the more spiritual view is chiefly connected with the name of Origen. It is thus sometimes called the 'Alexandrian' view. But it can hardly be correctly limited by such a designation; for Origen based himself directly on Paul, and indirectly on many a philosopher and mystic who was not of Alexandria.

Unfortunately this great thinker's treatise on the resurrection is lost. But from a Letter of Jerome to Pammachius,[2] we can recover a passage from Book iv. which is highly instructive.[3]

[1] '*Resurget igitur caro, et quidem omnis, et quidem ipsa, et quidem integra.*' – *De Carn. Res*, 59, ed. Kroyman, 1906 *Corp. Scriptt. Latt.* (Acad. Vind.), vol. 47.

[2] *Ep. s. Hieron.* 38 *ad Pammach.*

[3] C. Ramers, in his *Des Origenes Lehre von der Auferstehung der Fleisches* (Trier, 1851), is hard put to it to reconcile this passage with his interpretation of isolated statements found elsewhere in Origen's works. For a sketch of the history of the subsequent con-

Origen, Jerome tells us, called the holders of the materialistic view *'simplices'*, *'philosarcas'* ('flesh-lovers'), *'innocentes et rusticos'*, – in Greek of course. This would seem almost to indicate that they could not then have been a very important body in the Christian world.

Origen, however, was equally opposed to another extreme view which, he avers, would have it that the resurrection-body was to be of a purely phantasmal nature – the theory of extreme 'docetism'.

This, he declares, was the view of a number of the Gnostic schools; though we doubt whether it can be fairly stated quite so crudely. In some respects these Gnostics seem to have held views on this subject very similar to those of Origen himself.

What, Origen begins by asking, is the use, in the resurrection, of a body of flesh, blood, sinews, and bones, of limbs and organs for functions of the flesh, such as eating and drinking, excretion and procreation? Are we to continue to do all these things for eternity?

The promise is far otherwise. Neither the matter nor the form will be the same.

There is, however, a real *continuum* of individuality, a substantial ground of personal identity.

Hidden in the seed of the tree is the principle (*ratio*,

troversy see 'The Resurrection-Body: A Study in the History of Doctrine', in *The Church Quarterly Review* (April 1909), lxviii.138-163.

logos) of the tree. This is the formative power (*virtus*, *dynamis*) in the seed, the spermatic principle, which is called symbolically in Greek *spinthērismos*.

What the precise meaning of this last term may be is difficult to say, for the lexicons are silent. It means, literally, 'emission of sparks', 'sparking'.

'Light-spark', or 'light-emanation', as is well known, is used by a number of Gnostic schools as a symbolic expression for the 'germ' of the spiritual man.

By Origen, however, it is used generally as the invisible principle of the visible seed – that which determines the nature of the visible seed.

It seems to be conceived of as a 'substantial' something; for in it, in the case of human bodies developed from this germinal ground, is said to inhere the immemorial principles of resurrection.

It is likened to the innermost part or 'pith' of plants; and is called by Origen, in the case of man, the 'nursery' or 'seed-plot' (*seminarium*) of the dead; that is, the ground from which they will rise.

It is the substance of many bodily forms for man, or the essence of human embodiment, and not only of the body of flesh.

The body of the resurrection, according to Origen, is to be of a supernal spiritual nature. Indeed elsewhere he calls it 'divine'.

'Another body, a spiritual and aetherial one, is promised us – a body that is not subject to physical touch, nor seen by physical eyes, nor burdened with weight, and which shall be metamorphosed according to the variety of regions in which it shall be. . . .

'In that spiritual body the whole of us will see, the whole hear, the whole serve as hands, the whole as feet.'

It will be a radical change of *schēma*, or plan, says Origen, quoting Paul.

If the stories of the risen body of Jesus being sensible to touch and eating food are here objected, Origen replies that the Master made it appear so in order to strengthen the faith of the doubting disciples.

From this time onwards the controversy became more and more embittered.

Speaking very roughly, and bearing in mind a number of exceptions on either side, the materialistic interpretation dominated the Western or Latin and the spiritualistic the Eastern or Greek Church.

After hesitation Augustine in the West adopted in its full sense the physical view. By the time of Gregory the Great, at the end of the sixth century, this had become so firmly established that the philosophical Eastern interpretation could safely be condemned as utterly heretical.

And so it continued throughout the middle ages.

Though the Reformers rejected the dogma of transubstantiation in the Eucharistic sacrament as being, in spite of the subtleties of the schoolmen, of a too material nature, they nevertheless strangely enough took over practically without question the naïve physical view of the nature of the resurrection-body.

Thus Article IV of the Anglican Church, in complete accord with Tertullian, reads: 'Christ did truly rise again from the dead, and took again his body, with flesh, bones, and all things appertaining to the perfection of man's nature.'

Of more recent years, however, with the application of an improved method to biblical study and a better knowledge of the history of the evolution of dogma, the pendulum has been swinging strongly in the direction of a more spiritual and philosophical view.[1]

Indeed it is not too much to say that it is difficult for some of us to meet with anyone of culture now-a-days who believes in a crude physical resurrection. The purely rationalistic treatment of miracles, however, based on the prejudices of an exclusively materialistic view of science, which has played so prominent a part in 'liberal theology' during the latter half of the nineteenth century, is no longer in fashion.

Latterly there have been marked signs of a desire in religious circles to reconsider the whole question

[1] See the interesting and instructive paper by Firmin Nicolardot, 'La Résurrection de Jésus et la Critique depuis Reimarus,' in Revue de l'Histoire des Religions, tom. lix., no. 3 (Mai-Juin, 1909), pp. 318-332. R. died in 1768. His notes on the subject were first published among other fragments of his writings by Lessing, at Wolfenbüttel, in 1777.

by the light of an improved psychology, which shall endeavour to take all the facts of human experience into consideration without prejudice.

A scientific psychology of religious experience is being inaugurated. The data of psycho-physical and psychical phenomena are being busily collected, both from present experience and from the accounts of similar experience in the past; and these data are being submitted to a searching analysis.

It is abundantly evident to all who have followed such enquiries without prejudice, that the study of similar varieties of psychical religious experience is a necessary preliminary to considering adequately any theory of the nature of the resurrection-body.

Moreover, the analysis of the New Testament documents touching the nature of the risen body of Jesus shows us that already in the beginning there was a strong difference of opinion.

In spite of all efforts at harmonisation, there is little doubt that the general intention of the Synoptic writers and the general view of the Pauline documents are at open variance.

The intention of the Synoptic evangelists is plainly to lay stress on the physical reality of the risen body. The retention of the stories of the empty tomb, the taking of food, etc., all indicate the anxiety to make it clear that the body that was raised was the identical body that suffered death.

In the fourth gospel (xx.14, xxi.4), however, the

stories of the difficulty of recognition and of complete non-recognition, and in the appendix to Mark (xvi. 12) of a changed form, indicate quite as clearly another view.

The belief in the resurrection of the actual physical body was by no means the belief of the majority of the Jewish populace of the time.

Nevertheless the orthodox Rabbis presumably were compelled to hold that a living physical body could ascend or be taken to heaven; for the scriptures affirmed that the bodies of Enoch and Moses and Elijah had so been taken up.

Still further, they believed that the miracle of revival, of restoration to life of the dead, had been wrought through Elijah, Elisha and Ezekiel.

Indeed we learn from the Talmuds, that belief in such wonder-working not only extended to what had been done in the past, but that it was held to be a present possibility. It was one of the main articles of Pharisaic faith.

Of the seven classes of Pharisees the most holy were those who were Pharisees from pure love to God.[1] For these Hasīdīm, or Pious, there was a gradual growth in holiness, or sanctity, of ten degrees the tenth stage being the power of prophecy. But even beyond this there was the consummation of the spiritual powers of healing the sick and raising the dead.[2]

---

[1] *Jer. Berachoth*, ix. 5; cp. *Sotah*, v. 5.
[2] *Bab. Aboda Sara*, 20a. There are no less than five recensions of

The early Jewish Christians of every grade, then, it is to be supposed, should have been aware of the similarity between the works of revival and the ascension-wonders related of the ancient prophets and those claimed on behalf of Jesus. Yet, apparently, they held that the resurrection of the body of Jesus was absolutely unique.

If we ask in what this wide difference consisted, the reply of conservative traditional scholarship is practically that all the statements of the gospels are to be taken as equally authentic and authoritative.

In the case of the revival wonders, they aver, the dead who were restored to life were restored to the identical body subject to all its previous conditions.

But in the case of the resurrection of Jesus the body was the same yet not the same. Generally speaking it was identical; but in some ways it was released from material conditions – e.g. it could pass through closed doors.

It might here be objected that the body of Elijah was equally the same and yet not the same.

Indeed there is no question of identity at all; for Elijah had not died.

That, however, his body was in some way released from material conditions is to be understood; for he

this *boraitha*, two in the Jer. and two in the Bab. Talmud, and one in *Midrash Rabba*. This tends to prove that the tradition is ancient, and Jellinek, a high Talmudic authority, unhesitatingly declares that it is a description of Essenism.

is related to have been taken to heaven in a chariot of fire.

If, on the other hand, we seek the aid of a more liberal criticism, we find that the frankly material elements of the resurrection-narratives are rejected as unhistoric.

It may be objected by believers in the absolute historicity of the whole of the narratives that this is an *a priori* judgment.

That, however, is more or less true whatever view is taken. It is indeed difficult to see how the writers of the New Testament documents also, with the possible exception of Paul, who reports his experience at first hand, can be fairly excluded from this disability.

It is, therefore, necessary to inform ourselves as to the views of the contemporaries of the earliest Jewish Christians and of the evangelists on the subject of the resurrection.

As has been already said, the belief of the populace was presumably largely of a material nature. The general resurrection was to be a return to life under physical conditions in order to participate in the Messianic kingdom on earth.

But the grossest form of this expectation was entertained only by the most ignorant, and cannot fairly be attributed even to the mass of the people, for more spiritual views had already spread far and wide.

Among the Ḥasīdīm and Essenes, among the cultured of the Pharisees (this is specially to be seen among apocalyptic writers who were strongly influenced by Persian ideas), such out-and-out materialistic views had long been abandoned. It is then exceedingly probable that more popular views also had undergone considerable change in the last century B.C.

Referring to the general development during this period of eschatological ideas, that is of belief in the 'latter things' – the end of the world and of man – Professor Charles, than whom we have no greater authority, tells us (*En. Bib.*, 'Eschat.') that:

'The hope of an eternal Messianic kingdom on the present earth is all but universally abandoned. The earth as it is, is manifestly regarded as wholly unfit for the manifestation of this kingdom.'

The views of the last century B.C. on the resurrection show a great development on those of the preceding century. With some the resurrection is to be entirely spiritual; with others there is to be a resurrection of the body of the righteous, only this 'body' is to be a garment of light, and those who possess it are to be angelic.

With the first centry A.D. 'the transcendent view of the risen righteous becomes more generally prevalent. The resurrection involves the "spirit" alone; or, the righteous are to rise vestured with the glory of God, or with their former body, which is forthwith to be transformed and made like that of the angels.'

Alexandrian writers and the Essenes not only held the more spiritual view of the resurrection, but also that, instead of awaiting the resurrection in Sheōl (Hadēs), 'the entrance of the righteous spirit on a blessed immortality is to follow on death immediately.'

Here then we have a variety of views, from the gross materialism of the populace to the high spiritualism of the mystics and religio-philosophers.

The view the Synoptic writers most strongly favour is in consonance with the crudest belief of the people.

The doctrine of the body of glory is the doctrine of Paul. It was no doubt confirmed in him by his own personal experience in his vision of the Master.

We know how strongly opposed Paul was to the 'after the flesh' doctrine. He himself at any rate made no attempt to 'harmonize' himself with it.

Paul's doctrine as to the resurrection-body is summarised by Professor Charles as follows:

'This present body is psychical as an organ of the psyche or "soul", just as the risen or spiritual body is an organ of the "spirit".

'Thus as the psychical body is corruptible, and clothed with humiliation and weakness, the spiritual body will enjoy incorruptibility, honour and power.

'Hence between the bodies there is no exact continuity. The existence of the one depends on the death of the other.

'Nevertheless there is some essential likeness between them. The essential likeness proceeds from the fact that they are successive expressions of the same personality, though in different spheres. It is the same individual vital principle that organises both.'

If then among cultured and mystic Hebrews there were high views of the resurrection-body, equally so among the better informed of the early Christians are similar views found.

Not only Paul but many other early Christian mystics, notably the Gnostics, held views that we can hardly doubt were based on experience, and which seem to throw light on the problem.

Now it is to be noted that Tertullian (*D. R. C.* 19) is specially annoyed with those whom he opposes (*pars diversa*), because they say the resurrection is to be taken in a spiritual sense. These he stigmatises as allegorists, and contends that they would make it all a purely figurative thing.

They say, he asserts, 'that "death" is really not the separation of body and soul but ignorance of God, whereby the man being dead to God lies buried in error as though in the grave.' Not only so, they say, but 'that the only resurrection worth considering is when on the coming of truth the man, reanimated and made alive again by God, casting off the death of ignorance, bursts forth from the grave of the "old man", for the Lord himself likened the Scribes and Pharisees to "whitened sepulchres".

'Whence it follows that they who have attained the

resurrection of faith, are with the Lord when they have put Him on in baptism.'

Tertullian, who was himself subsequently condemned for the 'heresy' of Montanism, characterises such beliefs as the 'mysteries of heretics' (*arcana haeretica*). They seem, however, in their general outlines, not to have been secret teachings, but widely proclaimed; for he continues:

'Indeed the majority (*plerique*), though claiming that there is a resurrection of the soul after its departure [from the body], interpret the coming forth from the grave as escaping from the "world", inasmuch as the "world" is the dwelling place of the "dead" – that is, of those who know not God; or even as the escape from the body itself, because the body also like a grave keeps the soul shut up in the death of the worldly life.'

But for the spiritually experienced this was a very real happening and not an arbitrary interpretation, as Tertullian would have it. In some schools indeed it was associated with the first true initiation into the *arcana* of the spiritual life.

If, for instance, we interpret the short passage of Irenaeus (I.xxiii.5) which summarizes the teachings of the Gnostic Menander, by the light of recent religio-historical research and by what we know generally of the nature of the main psychology of the Gnostic schools, the view of 'the majority' will be more clearly seen.

Menander, who was strongly imbued with Chaldaeo-Magian mystery-lore, and stood on the borderland between it and general Christian doctrines, taught that the chief end of the gnosis was the overcoming of the 'world' and its 'rulers'. This could be achieved only by means of the 'resurrection', that is to say, by being brought into immediate contact with the Saving Power through one in whom that Spirit was already active, by means of a baptism which must have been of a spiritual nature. For it was believed to bestow upon the recipient an earnest of immortality and of eternal youth; and this could not very well apply to the physical body.

The clearest form of the teaching to which Tertullian refers, however, is to be found in the composite Naassene Document quoted by Hippolytus (v. 7ff.).[1]

Speaking of the primal Spiritual Man, the Pagan commentator (who is certainly pre-Christian) of the Greek mystery-hymn that forms the text of the whole exposition, tells us that this Immortal Man is buried in mortal man.

We learn further (§ 8) that, in their mystery-teaching, 'the Phrygians call Him also Dead – when buried in the body as though in a tomb or sepulchre.'

On this the Christian Gnostic writer, who years afterwards commented on the Pagan and Jewish

---

[1] For the analysis of this document, see my *Thrice-greatest Hermes*, i.142ff.

commentators who had preceded him, adds two quotations either from some lost Gnostic gospel, or – can it possibly be? – even from a lost collection of Sayings, as follows:

'This is what is said:

' "Ye are whited sepulchres, filled with the bones of the Dead",[1] for Man, the Living One, is not in you.

'And again He says:

' "The Dead shall leap forth from their graves"[2] – that is, from their earthly bodies, regenerated, spiritual, not fleshly.

'This is the Resurrection that takes place through the Gate of the Heavens, through which all those who do not pass remain Dead.'

We thus see that the resurrection is equated with the new birth or birth from above, the spiritual birth out of or through the pure virgin substance into the consciousness of immortality.

The Pagan commentator continues: 'The same Phrygians again call this very same [Man or man], after the transformation, God [or a god].'

And on this the Christian writer notes: 'For he becomes God when, rising from the Dead, through such a Gate, he shall pass into Heaven.'

The mystery of 'divinising' (*apotheōsis*) or 'transcending death' (*athanasía*) was not, however, to be deferred to *post-mortem* existence, though it had to be

---

[1] Cp. what underlies Mt. xxiii.27, Lk. xi.44 and Acts xxiii.3.
[2] Cp. what underlies Mt. xxvii.52, 53.

preceded by a mystical death. It was a mystery wrought in the living body of a man.

With such spiritual rites and operations the members of most of the Christian Gnostic schools seem to have been familiar. What, however, many of them sought to do was to introduce a unique element in the case of Jesus. But here naturally there was much earnest debate.

Thus we are told that even in one and the same school opinion was divided as to the mystery of the spiritual resurrection in the case of Jesus. The widespread Valentinian movement was so divided.

In its Western tradition (Hipp., vi.35) Jesus was said to have had, like all men, a psychic body, that is a 'fleshly', mortal vehicle of the soul. The 'resurrection from the dead' was operated by the baptism of the Spirit. The popular story of the descent of the dove signified the descent of the Spirit, which they regarded in this connection as the Logos or Supernal Wisdom. The descent of the Spirit was the resurrection or coming to life and consciousness in the mortal man of the Spiritual Man.

The Eastern tradition, on the other hand, refined the uniqueness of Jesus to the utmost. They contended that the body of Jesus already from birth was the spiritual body. Now though this 'body' from one point of view was the most real of all substantial things, from the physical standpoint it was an 'appearance', and therefore the Eastern

Valentinians were regarded as extreme 'docetists'.

In brief, it may be said that all the Gnostic schools repudiated the doctrine of a fleshly resurrection, and centred their interest in a more immediate and spiritual interpretation of the mystery.

When we say 'spiritual', however, it is of course not to be supposed that this means a condition of things absolutely removed from all possibility of manifestation; that is, spiritual in an absolute sense, as entirely divorced from everything other than it-self, if such a thing be possible.

According to Paul the 'spiritual' body is not a body of pure spirit, which would be, philosophically speaking, an absolute contradiction in terms; but a body capable by its purity of manifesting the im-mediate power of the Spirit.

This, the 'fleshly', psychic body, he believed, could not do. The spiritual body was a 'glory', a body of power.

In the Gnostic post-resurrectional Gospel, known as *Pistis Sophia*, we have a magnificent description of the perfect body of glory of the Master, the vesture of light, which is practically the vehicle of all the supernal powers of the Universe.

In the Syrian Gnostic *Hymn of the Soul*, or *Hymn of the Pearl*, the robe of glory is sealed with the names or powers of the divine hierarchy from the King of kings downwards.

Many of these sublime descriptions are, no doubt,

largely conditioned by the feeling that the physical body is a thing of dishonour or, at any rate, of humiliation.

But this cannot really be so as viewed in the greater life. And so, in spite of the crudity of the belief in the resurrection of the actual physical body, there seems to be at the back of it the dim intuition of a certain great truth – namely, that the *whole* man must embrace the corporeal as well as the psychic, the mental and the spiritual.

Did the mystics then believe that there was an absolute divorcement in every sense between the physical or material vehicle and the 'spiritual body' of the resurrection? It seems already pretty evident that they did not do so.

Tertullian's contention that the interpretation he opposes is merely what might be termed the 'reification' of a metaphor, or even at best an immaterial moral regeneration, as many may regard it to-day, is not, apparently, what was believed.

Most of the Gnostics, at any rate, held that in the spiritual rebirth something most real in all senses, some *substantial* as well as moral change, was wrought in them.

If we read them aright, they believed that, with truly spiritual 'repentance,' or the 'turning-back' of the whole nature to God, that is with effective moral regeneration, the actual body or ground of resurrection was substantially brought to birth in them.

Was this, then, simply some subtle body of identical or even somewhat changed physical form, capable of manifesting more extended powers than the 'flesh'?

Yes and No. It was not *a* body in any order of subtle bodies in immediate sequence with the physical body, of which so much is heard among the psychics of all ages. It was rather the source of every possibility of embodiment – the germ-ground, or *seminarium*, from which all such bodies could be produced.

Now some have attempted to interpret the dogma of the resurrection of the physical body according to the belief in reincarnation; and so would have the resurrection-body to be the 'again-rising of the flesh' in the form of a new physical body in a subsequent physical life.

It is true that many of the Christian as well as Pagan Gnostic schools believed in transmigration, or transcorporation.[1] They held, however, that the body of the resurrection was a body of freedom and not a body of bondage. The great change wrought at the resurrection was fundamental. It freed man from the constraints of 'fate', from the dominion of the 'rulers'.

[1] It may be of interest here to note in correction of certain popular but erroneous statements which are becoming very prevalent, that the Church Fathers did not in any case 'teach reincarnation'. A few, like Origen, put forward the doctrine of the pre-existence of the soul. But Origen explicitly and vigorously condemns the doctrine of transmigration or transcorporation, the characteristic dogma of the reincarnationists.

Fortunately we possess a mystery-ritual, or rather the ritual of a mystic rite of personal religion, that gives us clear indications of the direction in which we should look to envisage the nature of this resurrection-body. It purports to be the innermost rite of the Mithriaca, and reference has already been made to it in the proem.

From it we learn that the 'perfect body' was fundamentally quintessential. It was primarily differentiated into simple subtle elements; whereas the physical body was conditioned by the gross mixed elements.

It is by means of this 'perfect body' that the new birth into immortality is consummated. That this is so may be seen from the opening invocatory utterance of the ritual, which runs as follows:

'O Primal Origin of my origination; Thou Primal Substance of my substance; First Breath of breath, the breath that is in me; First Fire, God-given for the Blending of the blendings in me; First Fire of fire in me; First Water of my water, the water in me; Primal Earth-essence of the earthy essence in me; Thou Perfect Body of me! . . .

'If, verily, it may seem good to you, translate me, now held in my lower nature, unto the Generation that is free from Death.

'In order that, beyond the insistent Need that presses on me, I may have Vision of the Deathless Source, by virtue of the Deathless Water, by virtue of the Deathless Solid, and by virtue of the Deathless Air.

'In order that I may become re-born in Mind; in order that I may become initiate, and that the Holy Breath may breathe in me.

'In order that I may admire the Holy Fire; that I may see the Deep of the [New] Dawn, the Water that doth cause the Soul to thrill; and that the Life-bestowing Aether which surrounds all things may give me Hearing.'[1]

The above are but a few rough notes on a theme of intense interest and enormous importance. They might be largely added to and developed to very considerable length.

I should, however, like to add a paragraph from Kohler's article on the 'Resurrection' in the *Jewish Encyclopaedia*, which may be of interest for those who are unacquainted with the state of affairs in reformed Judaism.

'In modern times the belief in resurrection has been greatly shaken by natural philosophy, and the question has been raised by the Reform rabbis and in rabbinical conferences whether the old liturgical formulas expressing the belief in resurrection should not be so changed as to give clear expression to the hope of the immortality of the soul instead.

'This was done in all the American Reform prayer-

[1] Dieterich (A), *Eine Mithrasliturgie* (Leipzig, 1903); see my *A Mithriac Ritual* (London, 1907).

books. At the rabbinical conference held at Philadelphia it was expressly declared that the belief in the resurrection of the body has no foundation in Judaism, and that belief in the immortality of the soul should take its place in the liturgy.'

May we venture to hope that Christian ecclesiastics also may be no less courageous in setting their house in order, even if they do not, as we hope they will not, go so far as the Reform rabbis in rejecting entirely all notion of a resurrection-body. There seems to be another way out, as we have tried to indicate.

Epilogue

Whoever has read so far, has now before him the three sketches which illustrate the main purpose of our thesis.

This purpose was to outline the most characteristic features of the doctrine of the subtle body as it was limned by those old masters of philosophic and mystic lore who were held in highest repute in Western classical antiquity, and whose views we may still regard with respect.

The treatment in detail stands out from the roughly washed-in background of the proem, which is intended solely to suggest the vast expanse of the general subject and the dim distances back to which it stretches.

The whole is a booklet and not a volume, an essay and not a treatise. The severest economy of treatment has had to be exercised in all respects, and great watchfulness to be maintained to prevent the pen running off into many a tempting disquisition.

And indeed it is not always an easy matter to decide what is subordinate and what is essential in pursuing the intricacies and unravelling the complexities of a subject so little surveyed in our own days, and of which the values have been as yet so superficially considered as the subtle embodiment of the life of the mind.

I fear I have but scanty skill in popular exposition and no gift for descriptive writing; but I have tried to remember throughout that the subject is intensely human, and as such of no little interest for the general reader as well as for the philosopher and scientist and the student of the comparative history of religion.

Sufficient indications have, I hope, been given for the learned to pursue the matter for themselves, should they be minded to do so. Many of them are so much better equipped technically than myself for the spade-work of the task that they could, if they would, turn out most valuable contributions on special points and define many a subordinate problem with a clarity that would go half way to its solution.

The general reader, however, is not a specialist and but little minded to appreciate the labours of technical research. Indeed the detailed work of specialists, and most of all the unattractive form in which it is almost invariably presented, scare him away at the very first sight as a matter of no interest for his immediate needs, and as having no bearing on his daily life.

I hope I have not frightened any away by the modicum of reference and annotation with which this booklet is equipped, and which may be so easily skipped.

Above all I have had in mind those ever increasing numbers who in very various and popular ways are having their attention drawn to certain classes of phenomena of a psychical nature, which are occurring to-day in manifold multiplicity. These are, generally speaking, as old as the world; yet the uninstructed regard most of them as startling novelties.

On all sides we are hearing of telepathy, telergy, clairvoyance, clairaudience, psychometry, mesmerism, hypnotism, suggestion and auto-suggestion, automatic writing, trance-phenomena, mediumship of every variety, multiple personality, exteriorisation of sensibility, psychical materialization, communication with the departed, visions and raps, dream-psychology, the psychology of the abnormal, with all its manifold complexities and well-nigh inexhaustible data, psycho-analysis, psychical research, psycho-therapeutics, mental and spiritual healing of every kind, and so on and so forth.

The atmosphere is thick with rumours of psychism, spiritism, theosophy, occultism, Christian science, new thought, magic and mystery and mysticism of every grade.

The dead have come forth from their tombs and the veil of the temple is rent once again in these days of catastrophic upheaval.

In scientific circles also, what is now known as the new psychology has been forced to take notice of some at any rate of the supranormal phenomena underlying all this psychical ferment. An impression is being slowly made even upon the nineteenth century type of mind that is still so influential in official circles.

Now, in my opinion, it is precisely this leading notion of a subtle body, which for so many centuries has played the dominant role in the traditional psychology of both the East and the West, that is most deserving of being retried, reviewed and revised, to serve as a working hypothesis to co-ordinate and explain a very large number of these puzzling psychical phenomena.

It is being already frankly so employed by a number of competent students outside the ranks of those who arrogate to themselves the status of being the only genuine representatives of official science, and it is eagerly accepted by hosts of people who make no pretence to any technical scientific proficiency, but who have had first-hand experience of some of the phenomena.

Many, if not most, of the latter are under the impression they are accepting a new notion, dealing with a new discovery. I hope, however, that those few of them who may chance to read this essay, may be persuaded that, so far from this being the case, they are simply being convinced today by personal experience of the legitimacy of one of the oldest persuasions of mankind.

It is true that science must advance slowly, and that this advance must be of a corporate nature. Science must rigidly test every step it takes by the most careful procedure it can command, before it can be sure its feet are planted on safe ground.

For my part, however, I cannot see how this particular step is so hazardous even for the irreconcilable foes of everything they cannot test physically by the most normal avenues of sense.

For those who take up so intransigeant an attitude however, I venture to think, the subtle body theory will always prove to be a potent presence haunting the threshold of that materialism from which in the belief of its devotees all superstition, as they deem it, has forever been banished. For this hypothesis comes into operation immediately with the patently physical phenomena of mediumship which supply psychical research with its most objective stratum of material.

But this lowest or most external grade of its manifestation is only the bottom rung of a ladder which, as we have seen, was believed with much show of reason by some of the greatest intellects and saintly characters of the past to rise aloft to heights of great sublimity.

The path of this interior ascent is an ever purer way of life that leads the soul at last on to that plain of truth where science and philosophy and religion, not only join hands, but blend into a single unitary gnosis that enables man to know himself in the perfect fulness of the presence of his God.

Other titles currently available from
Solos Press

Hermetica

the writings attributed to

Hermes Trismegistus

Edited and translated
by
Walter Scott

The *Hermetica* is the name given to an extraordinary collection of writings ascribed to Hermes Trismegistus, the Greek name for the legendary teacher, prophet and scribe deified by the Egyptians as the god Thoth and known to the Hebrews as Enoch. When in about 1460 AD a Greek manuscript of the *Corpus Hermeticum* came into the possession of Cosimo de Medici, Duke of Florence, he ordered Marsilio Ficino to leave aside the works of Plato and concentrate instead on these 'lost works of Hermes'.

Later scholarship indicates that these writings are not as old as was thought, in fact they probably date from only the second and third centuries AD. However, they are clearly the work of an esoteric school involved in self-development and it is very likely that this school belonged to a tradition going back to the earlier Egypt of Hermes.

The *Hermetica* can be studied from many different angles. They were a source of inspiration to C.G. Jung when he was developing his system of depth psychology, they are clearly one of the main sources of Gudjieff's cosmology and they are in close

ISBN   1-873616-02-3 (Paperback) £12.95
       1-873616-04-X (Hardback) £19.95